Mercedes For The Road

By Henry Rasmussen

MERCEDES FO

Published by Motorbooks International
Publishers and Wholesalers, Inc.
Osceola, Wisconsin, U.S.A.
Copyright 1983 by Henry Rasmussen.
ISBN 0-87938-191-4.
Library of Congress number 83-8124.
Printed in Hong Kong by
South China Printing Company.

The 220 was the first new body style from Mercedes-Benz after the war. The old 170, although similar, had been introduced in 1936, and then reintroduced in 1946 when postwar production started again. The classic grille was retained on the 220, but the headlights were now mounted inside the fenders instead of on top of them. The six-cylinder overhead cam engine displaced 2195cc, had one Solex carburetor and gave 80hp at 4850rpm. Acceleration from 0-60 took about twenty-one seconds. Top speed was 90mph. The Cabriolet came in two styles: A) Front seats only, without rear quarter windows; and B) Front and rear seats with rear quarter windows. The wheelbase was 112 inches and 6.40X15-inch tires were used.

Both the Sedan and the Cabriolets were introduced in 1951. The last Cabriolet in the series was made in 1955. A total of 2,360 220A and 220B Cabriolet were built. A hardtop Coupe was made available in 1954. The 220 received a new body in 1954 — known as the 220a only available as a sedan.

The original 220 frame was shaped like an X and made of oval tubes. Fully independent suspension was utilized. The transmission was fully synchronized, had four speeds, and had the lever mounted on the steering wheel column. The price in the United States was just over $5,000.

The styling of the 220A Cabriolet was not as dramatic as that of the 300S. Nevertheless, the engineering and the workmanship was excellent, carrying forward the classic Mercedes-Benz tradition.

A modern interpretation of the famous prewar 540K, the 300S model was at once prestigious and sporty. It was first shown at the Paris Salon in 1951. *Road & Track* supplemented a road test of the 300 Sedan version by saying, "breathes there an enthusiast, who after driving a superb piece of machinery, has not started dreaming of modifications? A little more power. A little lightening of the body here and there. A touch of this and that to add to the sporting characteristics." The S model was the answer!

The 300S was made from 1952 till 1955. The 300Sc — small letter "c" signifying production modifications — was made from 1955 till 1958. The Sc was similar to the S, but had fuel injection and single-pivot swing axle. The X-shaped frame was mounted on a 114.2-inch wheelbase; the 2996cc straight six engine produced 175hp at 4300rpm and a top speed of 112mph; the 0-60 time was fourteen seconds. Only 200Sc units were built — in 1957 only fifty-two!

The external difference between the S and the Sc lay in two small areas — the rubber strips on the bumpers were eliminated and louvers were added to each side of the hood. At a price of $12,500 when introduced in New York, it was not your everyday utility runabout!

The superb quality that has become synonymous with the Mercedes-Benz name is everywhere evident on this model. With its conservative styling and high-quality craftsmanship, it has an aura of timeless elegance.

220A Cabriolet

300Sc Roadster

The 300SL Gullwing Coupe — with doors that open up instead of out — was born on the racetrack. The unorthodox manner of access was necessary because of the side-members of its advanced multi-tube frame. The wheelbase of 94.5 inches would be repeated on the 190SL and the later 230-250-280SL Roadsters. Independent suspension is the rule for Mercedes-Benz automobiles. The 300SL engine is the same 2996cc straight six-cylinder that powered the rest of the 300 series. With Bosch fuel injection, power was 240hp at 5800rpm. Top speed was about 140mph with 60mph reached in about 7.4 seconds. A four-speed transmission, with synchromesh in all gears was used. Tire size was 6.70X15. The production 300SL Coupe was introduced in 1954 and was replaced by the 300SL Roadster in 1957. A total of 1,400 Coupes were built, with the majority of 867 built in 1955. The price at that time was $7,463.

After the many victories of the 300SL factory racing team in 1952, the production version was eagerly awaited. *Road & Track* said, "just when we were beginning to suspect that the 300SL Coupe would prove to be a mediocre performer, we got one for a full scale road test. The new car turned out to be far beyond our boldest expectations." The magazine finished the article by saying, "The sports car of the future is here today."

Few automotive creations have achieved the degree of visual impact as has the 300SL Gullwing, its powerful looking, yet elegant forms inspire admiration from enthusiasts and non-enthusiasts alike.

The 300SL Roadster was a definite improvement over the Coupe; it provided better all-around vision — and, of course, better ventilation — a shortcoming of the Coupe. Actually, the Roadster should be called a convertible, since it had roll-up windows. In late 1958, an optional hardtop became available and in March 1961 disc brakes became standard equipment.

The Roadster kept the basic tube-frame format of the Coupe, but it was modified to allow conventional doors. A new low-point swing axle improved handling. Independent suspension, six-cylinder, single overhead cam, three-liter engine with fuel injection, and four-speed transmission, remained. Power was up, 250hp at 6200rpm. Speed varied with rear axle ratio; *Road & Track* got a faster 0-60 time of seven seconds but a lower top speed of only 130mph with the Roadster compared to the Coupe. In a later test, the magazine said, "To those who can afford the initial cost it offers a car they can be proud of, and they will be secure in the knowledge that not many cars on the road are better built or can cover ground faster with as much safety."

A total of 1858 were built from 1957 to 1963 (only fractionally fewer Coupes were made). In 1958 only 324 were made; each costing $10,970. The Roadster did not have quite the charisma of the Coupe. The Gullwing was indeed a difficult act to follow, quickly creating an almost cult-like enthusiasm for itself. The Roadster was a more practical automobile than the Coupe — easier entrance and exit, slightly heavier but more powerful and with better handling.

300SL Coupe

300SL Roadster

Introduced at the same time as the 300SL, the 190SL was always outclassed by its big brother. Indeed, the 190SL was an altogether different automobile. Although it had the same wheelbase as the 300SL, 94.5 inches, it had unit construction derived from the 180 Sedan. The suspension was as on all Mercedes-Benz cars, independent all around. Thirteen-inch wheels were used.

Autocar tested a 190SL in 1958 and found that "The overall impression was one of comfort and of sparkling performance with a very reassuring level of safety. It is necessary to make full use of the well-designed four-speed gear box if maximum performance is to be obtained." Rightfully so, since the 190SL had a single overhead cam, four-cylinder engine displacing 1897cc. Power was 120hp at 5700rpm using dual Solex carburetors. Performance was 0-60 in thirteen seconds and a top speed of 102mph could be reached.

The 190SL was introduced in 1954, but 1955 was the first year of production. By the time the last one had been built in 1963, 25,881 units graced the roads worldwide — ample proof that Mercedes-Benz' marketing strategy worked. The price in 1955 was $3,998.

Conceived in the shadows of the 300SL, the 190SL has always remained there. The large numbers produced and its relatively sluggish performance collaborated to keep it there.

All of the side windows of the 300d could be lowered — the windows in the front and rear doors as well as the rear quarter window (the latter was lifted out) — creating an uninterrupted opening much like a prewar phaeton. Yet, it was not a primitive tourer — it was a formal limousine! The 300 series was the most exciting line of cars to come from any manufacturer in the fifties. Racing car, sports car, two-seat luxury tourer, distinctive limousine — they could all be found in the 300 series.

Introduced in 1951, the 300 Sedan stayed in production until 1962. The 300d Sedan was produced from 1957 till 1962. A total of 3,077 Sedans were built; in 1962 only 45 were made. A convertible was also available.

With a fuel-injected, six-cylinder engine displacing 2996cc, the power output was 180hp at 5300rpm. The wheelbase was an impressive 124 inches and 7.60X15 tires were used. Three-speed automatic transmission was standard. Performance included a top speed of 105mph and a 0-60 time of eighteen seconds. The price in the United States was approximately $10,000.

The frame was X-shaped, using oval tubes. But the styling of the 300d differed from the earlier 300 Sedans in several areas; the front fenders protruded farther forward and had larger rings around the headlamps; the rear fenders and the trunk were more pronounced; the rear quarter windows were enlarged. The 300 series finally brought all that prewar prestige back to Mercedes-Benz.

190SL Roadster

300d Sedan

There were two different body-style versions of the 220S and SE Cabriolets and Coupes. The style featured here was produced from 1958 to 1960; the later version from 1960 to 1965. The early model still carried a hint of rear fender in spite of the slab-side styling.

Powered by the overhead cam, six-cylinder engine of 2195cc, it produced 120hp at 4800rpm — the same as the later 220SEb. The 0-60 time was about fourteen seconds, with a top speed of 107mph. The "E" stood for "Einspritz" — fuel injection. The Bosch system was used.

These models all had unit bodies with traditional independent suspension and sat on wheelbases of 106.3 inches — some 4.7 inches shorter than the sedans. Four-speed transmission with the gear lever mounted on the steering column was standard on the 220 S and SE versions. Small, 6.70X13 tires were used. Price in the United States was about $8,500. Total production of 220S Coupes and Cabriolet was 3,429 units from 1956 to 1959; and of the 220SE, 1,942 from 1958-1960. The 1960 production was 1,200.

As a small concession to the current trend, the windshield curved back slightly. The distinctive grille raised with the hood when engine maintenance was due, rather awkward, but necessary. When the top was lowered and the boot installed, it presented a fairly flat look. This was something relatively new for German coachbuilding, especially on a touring model.

"The Mercedes 600 is not an ordinary car," said *Road & Track*. It went on to quote from the factory announcement that stated, "The new car takes up the prewar tradition of the company which was to have at least one model which would be included whenever ultra-prestige cars were considered." The magazine continued, "Its sheer bulk is imposing and because the mind's eye is not accustomed to such grand dimensions, it takes a while to encompass it — like a statue that is larger than life. Or a cathedral."

The 126-inch wheelbase is indeed enormous, but the 9.00X15 tires help to camouflage the size. The general looks of the car show the kinship to the regular Mercedes-Benz line. The makeup of the immense auto is also similar — independent suspension, low-pivot swing axle, unit construction, fuel injection — but the 600 goes beyond with a self-leveling suspension system, ground clearance and ride softness that could be adjusted by the driver, pneumatically operated windows lifts, seat adjustments, door locks, trunk lid and so on.

Power was by a V-8 engine with an overhead cam for each bank. It displaced 6329cc and produced 300hp at 4100rpm. In spite of the 5,434-pound weight, performance was rapid — to 60mph from a standstill took just ten seconds; top speed 127mph. In 1969, the price of the 600 Limousine was close to $21,000, and 279 were made that year.

The 600 series was introduced at the Frankfurt Auto Show in 1963. Until the end of 1979, 2,613 units had been produced.

220SE Cabriolet

600 Limousine

A convertible selling for more than $14,000, with a hand-operated top, styling from 1960 and a short 108.3-inch wheelbase — only Mercedes-Benz could do it and be successful! This was the 1971 280SE 3.5 Cabriolet. The 280SE Coupe and Cabriolet models carried the same body as the 250SE, which in turn carried the same body as the 220SEb of eleven years previous.

In the beginning it had the familiar six-cylinder, 2195cc, single overhead cam engine. Later, the enlarged 2496cc was fitted, as well as the fuel injected 2996cc unit, the car now being labeled 300SE. Later yet, it received the 2778cc engine before it was finally outfitted with the new 3.5 V-8 powerhouse in 1969. It produced 230hp at 6050rpm. Top speed was 127mph and 0-60 time was about nine seconds.

The suspension was the by now well-proven independent type front and rear, with the diagonal-pivot swing axle. Unit construction provided solid, rattle-free motoring. Tire size was 185H14. As always, included in every Mercedes-Benz was superior quality and solid engineering. It was done right, or it wasn't done at all.

But the 3.5 proved to possess another quality as well; the powerful 3.5 engine provided the final impetus to a model that had symbolized the utmost in styling and comfort for more than a decade — now it became an instant classic. Altogether, since its introduction in 1960, 36,000 Coupes and Cabriolets of the 220, 250, 300, 280 and 3.5 types were made — in 1971, only 1,026 units.

"The Mercedes-Benz 300SEL 6.3 holds the top honor among sedans because of its scorching performance that is blended with the usual traits of comfort, longevity and dignity. The best description of it is that it comes close to being all of the Ten Best Cars of the World in one great package." Those are the words of *Road & Track!* What more needs to be said?

In 1971, at $16,275, one could, of course, have expected more than a 112.8-inch wheelbase. But what fools these mortals be. Look at today's market and today's prices! The 6329cc V-8 put out the same 300hp at 4100rpm as the 600, but because of the lighter weight (3,828 pounds) performance was 6.9 seconds for 0-60 and top speed was 131mph. No wonder *Road & Track* labeled the performance "scorching." And no wonder that it concluded, "If we had to choose one car, regardless of cost, to serve all our automotive desires, it would have to be the 300SEL 6.3."

This fabulous sedan was produced from 1967 till 1972. In all, 6,526 units were made, just 670 in 1971. It was truly understated. The only way you could tell the 6.3 powerplant was to look for the small numerals on the trunk lid. *Road & Track,* in its road test, said, "But in every one of the lesser Mercedes, we've always felt a little apologetic for the lack of power. No so with the 6.3."

A gentleman's hot rod indeed, and today still surprisingly affordable.

280SE 3.5 Cabriolet

300SEL 6.3 Sedan

Tradition can be a Pavlovian kind of thing! It is doubtful that the 280SL ever won a road race — but it sure looked like it could. It had the lines of the 300SL, down to the grille. It even had the same wheelbase, 94.5 inches. At $7,469, in 1971, it sold only 830 units; but from 1967, when it replaced the 250SL, until the last 280SL was produced in 1971, it sold 23,885 units. Added to some 25,000 previously built 230SL and 250SL models it became another "right car for the right time!" Maintaining the Mercedes-Benz theme of unit construction, independent suspension, low-pivot swing axle and fuel injection, the personal-sized Mercedes again hit the spot. Powered by a 2778cc six-cylinder engine producing 180hp at 5700rpm, performance was a creditable 9.9 seconds 0-60. Top speed was 114mph with four-speed automatic transmission. The stick-shift might have taken a second off the 0-60 time.

The 230SL, 250SL and 280SL line continued the Mercedes theme of elegance mixed with sportiness; it would not be out of place at the yacht club or the supermarket. But, a Mercedes is first of all meant to be driven. *Road & Track* said, "The ride, over all sorts of roads, is fantastic. The body is absolutely rigid and rattle free, and the supple suspension just works away down there without disturbing the superb poise of the SL." The 230SL, 250SL and 280SL — already classics, already increasing in value.

The 3.5-liter 350SL could not be imported into the United States. The imported 350SL always had a 4520cc engine — a V-8 producing 190hp at 4750rpm. The California version produced only 180hp because of stringent smog regulations. Bosch fuel injection helped keep the carbon monoxide and nitrous oxide levels down. Performance was 10.2 seconds 0-60 and top speed was 124mph. The usual Mercedes-Benz arrangement of unit construction, independent suspension and diagonal-pivot swing rear axle were retained — but the 350SL and 450SL was an all-new design. It was heavier and longer than the 230SL, 250SL and 280SL models it replaced.

In 1977, the European market received the 450SL 5.0 with front and rear spoiler. Currently, the body houses the 3.8-liter engine in the United States and is known as the 380SL. The 450SL was introduced in 1971 and in 1974 its price was $17,056. Production that year was 6,093 units.

Road & Track compared the 450SL to four other roadsters. The 450SL was tested against the Corvette, Dino 246GTS, Jaguar E-Type V-12 and the Porsche 911 Targa. The testers pointed out, "these are five very different cars." It was a test with no winner intended. They said, "The 450SL is in a class by itself: not as we said, a sports car — but fast enough for almost anyone and a wonderful two-seater for someone who wants quality but not necessarily excitement." They also said, "it's a two seat luxury car for driving fast in supreme comfort and avoiding the bulk of a big sedan."

280 *SL Roadster*

450 *SL Roadster*

The Best or Nothing!

Although this is the eighth volume in The Survivors Series, I have never before done a book on a marque I have actually owned.

My first Mercedes was a 190SL that I acquired in 1967, while I still lived in Sweden. The second was a 250SE Cabriolet that I possessed for too short of a time, after I had moved to California.

Having owned Mercedes automobiles does not mean that I can claim to be well familiar with their inner workings; engineering was never my forte. It only means that I know firsthand what it *feels* like to *own* a Mercedes; I am referring to that special feeling — a blend of pride and invulnerability. and it means that I know what it feels likc to *drive* a Mercedes; anyone who has driven one will always remember that solid, tight, massive feeling transmitted through the steering wheel. It even means that I know what a Mercedes *smells* like; somewhat naively I brag about being able to tell a Mercedes apart from other automobiles while blindfolded inhaling the fragrance of the leather.

So, what makes Mercedes-Benz so special?

Well, they were the ones who started it all — the first to manufacture and market an automobile. No other car company has been around for so long, surviving both wars and oil gluts as well as depressions and recessions.

A tradition as long as theirs has come about as a result of — but has also helped dictate — a formula that has been followed in the creation of every new design. It is a formula that has produced sound engineering and dignified styling; a formula concerned with both safety and economy as well as comfort and elegance; a formula that is perfectly expressed in the company's own credo; The Best or Nothing!

The following pages endeavor to communicate the result of this formula, illustrating it impartially, with cold facts and photographs that do not exaggerate, but also — and may the reader forgive — partially, through the owners' and my own irrepressible enthusiasm. Enjoy!

One of the world's most recognized symbols, the Mercedes Star was first seen in 1909. The three points symbolize the threefold application of Daimler products – on land, at sea and in the air. The pictures on these pages illustrate a few of the many uses of the Mercedes Star. Above, it graces the rear deck of a 300SL. To the right, it crowns the radiator of a 300d. On the opposite page, it is seen incorporated in the 300SL grille. To the far right, it is imbedded into the horn button of a steering wheel, and below, it is seen as a part of the bodybuilder's badge on a 220A Cabriolet.

Mercedes designers always seem to succeed in creating interiors with just the right blend of function and elegance. Above, the racecar-inspired cockpit of a 300SL Roadster – a curving chrome strip outlines its inviting shape. Above right, the lounge-like cabin of a 300d Sedan – the wide seats are covered with smooth leather, the dash and windows lined with rich wood. To the right, a 280SE Cabriolet in the driveway leading to the suburban Chicago home of a wealthy publisher. Opposite page, a 220A Cabriolet on a dusty plantation road near Caracas, Venezuela. Far right, the snug airplane-like accommodations of a 300SL Gullwing.

Hub caps changed very little over almost three decades – illustrative of the conservative evolution of design at Mercedes. Above, the cap of a 1952 220A had a small diameter, covering only the hub. As was the style, it was painted the color of the car, leaving very little chrome showing. On a 1957 300Sc, right, and a 1962 300d, opposite page, the hub caps remained basically the same, but were now surrounded by separate vented chrome rings. On a 1960 220SE Cabriolet, far right, the restorer left the cap unpainted. On a 1974 450SL, the cap is a one-piece affair, covering the entire wheel. Throughout, the Star remained the decorative element.

F or sheer beauty, few headlight designs can compete with that of the European version 300SL Roadster, left. Its smoothly rounded shape seems to form the perfect beginning of the fender, but not only esthetically, also aerodynamically – Mercedes engineers never design things just to look good! The headlights of the 300SL Gullwing, upper right, had a conventional design. Pictured above and to the lower right, the headlights of the 280SL and the 300SE, both shown in their American versions. In the photograph to the far left, the classic headlight shape of the 300d Sedan.

Details make the whole – and attention to detail has always characterized a Mercedes. The pictures on these pages, although only a few, are evidence enough. From the studied shape of the door handle on a 300SE Sedan, to the harmonious symmetry of the gauges on the dash of a 300SL Gullwing, to the speed-evoking slant of the louvres in its body side vent, to the smooth curves of the wood and the intricate folds of the leather on the door panel of a 220SE Cabriolet, to the perfect fit of the chrome moldings around its windshield – it all shows that Mercedes never left up to chance the design of even the smallest detail.

Man and his machine — a reflection of the owner's personality. Opposite page, Alex Dearborn unveils his choice machine, a 300SL Gullwing. It peers out from behind the garage doors of a converted New England carriage house — old-world perfection. This page, far left, Jose Harth admires the flowing forms of this 300SC Roadster — flamboyant elegance. It is parked in the courtyard of an old Venezuelan hacienda. Above, Lee McDonald sits ready for take-off in his 190SL. The beams of a sinking Florida sun reach into an always-open cockpit — gallant audacity. Left, Jay Pettit makes himself at home in the backseat of his 300d — conservative class. The fertile plains of Illinois draw an uninterrupted horizon line.

Short Resumé of a Long History.

By Gene Babow.

"The sight of Stuttgart was heart-rending. No newspaper report could convey what the eyes beheld. I kept asking myself where the people I saw lived — the houses were almost all bombed out or damaged.

"The next morning I drove to Untertürkheim, to the factory. I found a field of rubble there. They were clearing the rubble away, everyone was shoveling and carrying off debris. All of the employees of the firm were helping, voluntarily and without pay, regardless of rank or position. 'Our' factory had to be rebuilt, 'our' star had to rise again."

This was how Rudolf Caracciola, perhaps the greatest of the Mercedes-Benz racing drivers, later described his reactions to seeing firsthand the terrible destruction caused by allied bombing raids during the final phase of World War II. Assessing their losses, the Board of Directors stated: "Daimler-Benz has ceased to exist."

But, miraculously, the "star" would rise again.

Adopted by the Daimler Company in 1909, the three-pointed star had already survived for almost four decades, including a world war and a great depression. The symbol was introduced nine years after founder Gottlieb Daimler's death. His two sons, who managed the company, chose the symbol, recalling that their father had once drawn a guiding star over a picture of his home in Deutz.

Daimler-Benz Aktiengesellschaft, which now manufactures Mercedes-Benz automobiles, trucks and buses, as well as engines used in all forms of transportation, is the ultimate result of a merger between "Daimler Motoren Gesellschaft" and "Benz and Cie" that took place in 1926.

Daimler had patented a small, light, high-speed engine in 1883. The same principle of design is still fol-

lowed today. Starting in 1886, Benz had begun manufacture of a two-stroke, stationary engine. It had gas-throttle control and enabled him to begin work on a self-powered vehicle. The same yer, Benz introduced his gas-engined vehicle. It was a three-wheeler, specially designed for the purpose — not a motor-powered horseless carriage. If Daimler's first effort, on the other hand, closely resembled the horseless carriage, it was because it actually was a converted horse-drawn carriage. Self-powered vehicles had been seen before Daimler and Benz' time. These two men, however, foresaw the future of the automobile and started actual production.

Just before his father's death in 1900, Paul Daimler had developed a small 8hp car. It had a honeycombed radiator up front and formed the basis for a new model, the Mercedes.

This new car was named after the daughter of a Daimler agent in southern France, Emil Jellinek. It was Jellinek who had proposed the new car, put up the money, and insisted on the name.

The new car had the engine up front, was lower and longer than its contemporaries, and had a more favorable power-to-weight ratio. These features would soon be copied by almost all automobile manufacturers.

The engineer responsible for the actual design of the Mercedes was Wilhelm Maybach. More than anyone else, it was Maybach who influenced Daimler to produce a complete automobile, rather than just engines for boats, trains and commercial vehicles.

Maybach was followed by Paul Daimler, who had inherited the engineering prowess from his father. At Benz, Hans Neibel was their counterpart.

In 1908, the Grand Prix of France was won by a Mercedes. The four-cylinder, 135hp car reached an average speed of 69mph. Benz cars were second and third. When Mercedes dropped out of racing, the Neibel-designed "Blitzen Benz" took over. Neibel even raced the car himself with notable success.

Mercedes came back in 1914 and won again, but the war put a damper on racing and development, especially at Mercedes and Benz. It took several years after the war, in 1923, before a four-cylinder, supercharged Mercedes was built. It ran at Indianapolis, but was not a winner. The development of this car was entrusted to an engineer from Austro-Daimler — Ferdinand Porsche. The following year, this same car won the Targa Florio. Porsche went on to develop the supercharged "K" sports car, as well as the legendary SS and SSK models.

When Porsche decided to open his own consulting

In 1945, at the end of World War II, much of Germany lay destroyed – the Mercedes plants included. But production was resumed already in 1946. The first units were similar to prewar models. To the left, an example of the 170-series is seen beside a ruin in an unidentified location – for our purpose it symbolizes past destruction and new beginnings. The 220-series was shown in 1949. It resembled the 170-line. By now foreign travel was again possible – a 220, above, is seen on the French Riviera. The 300-series, right, shown in 1951, was the first all-new postwar design.

firm, Hans Neibel became the chief engineer. Neibel specialized in suspension and chassis design. He was responsible for the 1934 Mercedes-Benz Grand Prix cars. Regrettably Neibel died before he could see the formidable success of his creations.

A part of this engineering period was Fritz Nallinger. In a Mercedes-Benz press release dated 1978, he was credited with "the application of independent suspension to all four wheels, friction free springs, self-supporting frame floor unit with sub-frame, high speed, light Diesel engine for trucks and autos and direct gasoline injection into the cylinder."

He also raced and, therefore, had a feel for cars that handled well. It was he who suggested the 300SL for 1952. He had also been instrumental in the creation of the 500K and 540K of the late thirties.

Enter Rudolf Uhlenhaut, the next generation Mercedes super-engineer. He was responsible for racing successes as well as improved passenger car handling and safety. Alfred Neubauer, director of competition at Daimler-Benz commenting on Uhlenhaut's contribution said, "Up until then [1937] every designer assumed that a racing car must be tightly sprung and noisy. As a result, drivers were tossed about like a dry martini in a cocktail shaker. Uhlenhaut introduced soft springs and a quieter engine. The new Mercedes was as comfortable as an easy chair with 600hp purring beneath it."

Although not a competition driver, Uhlenhaut's capacity behind the wheel has become a legend. An example often mentioned is the occasion when Juan Manuel Fangio tried out the W196 Grand Prix car at Nürburgring. Fangio was finally satisfied with his lap time, but Uhlenhaut was not. He went out and bettered the time, according to this account.

No history of Mercedes-Benz, however brief, could be complete without mentioning Alfred Neubauer, the team manager. He was a master of strategy and also introduced the signals between pit and driver.

Prewar production from 1936 until the outbreak of the war was about 90,000 of the Type 170, 20,000 Type 230 and 300 540K. In 1938 alone, automobile production totaled 27,762.

In 1946, it was time to pick up the pieces and start over again. At first, only repair work was done. Then the plant at Mannheim, which suffered the least damage, resumed commercial production.

In 1946, only 214 passenger cars were built. In 1947, production increased to 1,045 units. In 1948, came the currency reform which brought stability to the new German Republic. A total of 5,116 cars of the

170 models were produced that year.

Early in 1951, Mercedes wished to return to Formula One racing. The then current formula of 1.5-liter supercharged or 4.5-liter without supercharger, would run until 1954. Mercedes could not have a new design ready until 1953. It was meaningless to produce a car for just one year of racing. Neubauer tried to get the formula extended, but failed.

Nallinger then came to the rescue. "How would it be if we developed a sports model out of our latest passenger car, the 300?" he suggested. The resulting 300SL put Mercedes back in racing. But it was the new Formula One, the 2.5-liter unsupercharged, that Mercedes wished to compete in. The W196 was the result, with lattice-type tubular frame, eight-cylinder engine, and desmodronic valve gear. With Uhlenhaut, Neubauer and Fangio on the team, the W196 was a winner. When Fangio drove the car, he said, "From the very first test, I was sure that I had in my hands the perfect car, the sensational machine that drivers dream about all their lives." He won the first race that the W196 appeared in, in 1954, at Rheims, France. He also won the German, Swiss and Italian Grand Prix races that same year, along with the championship in 1954 and 1955.

Now a few words about nomenclature. The numbers used to label passenger car models usually referred to engine size; 170 was 1.7 liters, 220 was 2.2 liters. The lower-case (a, b, c and d) letters signified further development of a model. Upper-case (A, B and C) letters signified body style; the 220A was a two seater convertible, 220B had a rear seat and a rear quarter window. There were exceptions, however, especially when the V-8 engine was introduced. The SL in 300SL stood for super light or "super leicht" in German. The letter S usually meant super. The E stood for "einspritz," or fuel injection in English. L meant long. D was usually reserved for diesel. The letter C originally meant a two-seater convertible for four passengers, without rear quarter window; but was later used to denote coupe, as in the 250 series.

The styling of Mercedes-Benz automobiles can be characterized as "non-trendy." True, there were vestigal fins at one time, but they were quickly removed. "Form follows function" is perhaps the best way to describe Mercedes styling. Yet, there has always been instant identification of any Mercedes automobile.

In recent years, Mercedes styling and size has been copied by almost every automobile maker. But it is really not styling that has placed Mercedes ahead of much of its competition, it is the faithful adherence to

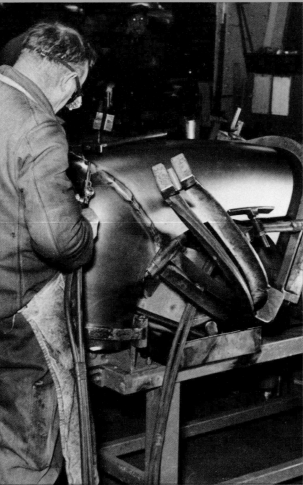

The pictures on these pages are from the early fifties, and show the Mercedes facilities bristling with activity. Note the absence of automation – the individual craftsman was king. To the left, the assembly area for the limited production covertibles. The profile in the foreground belongs to a 220A Cabriolet. Above, getting the piping of the seat just right requires careful attention. To the right, a fender takes shape. Top of the page, a 300-series engine is monitored while running on the test bed.

the meaning of the words safety and quality.

This book deals with the 1946 to 1974 models. At the end of that period, total annual production was 331,682. In the United States, 41,865 were sold through about 380 dealers. Prices ranged from $6,662 for the 220D to $16,498 for the 450SLC.

For comparison, the figures for 1981 show total production at 440,778. Sales in the United States totaled 63,059 through 409 dealers. Prices ranged from $21,858 for the 240D to $51,956 for the 380SEC.

Mercedes-Benz now ranks fifteenth in motor vehicle production, worldwide. Besides the factories in Stuttgart/Untertürkheim, Sindelfingen, Mannheim, Gaggenau and Berlin/Marienfelde, there are plants in Düsseldorf, Bad Homburg, Worth/Rhine, Munich, Friedrichshafen and Nürnberg. There are also assembly plants in Argentina, Brazil and Turkey.

The following is a brief look at the first three decades of Mercedes-Benz models with regard to their collectability. For the most part, the four-door sedans have been omitted. While these are fine automobiles, they were the plebeian transportation. Almost by definition, any two-door Mercedes-Benz will be collectable. The demand factor rates high. Simple economics dictate ever-increasing values.

170SA and 170SB Cabriolet. The Model 170 was first introduced at the Berlin Auto Show in 1936. The same design was also to become the mainstay of early postwar production at Mercedes-Benz, beginning in 1946. The last of the dozen or so variations on the 170 theme was built in 1955. Due to the relatively low production numbers of these cars, especially during the first years, the 170 in all its various forms, must to some extent be considered collectable. But it is particularly the A Cabriolet, the convertible two-seater, and the B Cabriolet, the convertible four-seater, that are desirable. A total of 2,433 between 1949 and 1951.

220A and B Cabriolet. Introduced at the Frankfurt Auto Show in 1951, the 2.2-liter sedans were the first new automobiles from Daimler-Benz after the war. These cars, along with the 220A and B Cabriolets and a later Coupe, still had fenders front and rear. Styling-wise, they were basically a facelift of the Model 170, with the headlights now in the fenders. Only 2,360 Cabriolets were made between 1951 and 1955. The Coupe came in 1954.

300a, b, c, d Sedan and Cabriolet. This prestigious line of automobiles was also introduced at the 1951 Frankfurt show. No attempt was made to join current styling trends; therefore, the model took a long time to become dated. Refined elegance was the

keynote. Obviously, the Cabriolets are the most rare — only 707 were made from 1951 to 1962. The total number of sedans built during the same period was 10,723. These automobiles were elegant and luxurious, but are not as sought-after today as their sportier two-seater counterparts, even though they were built with the same attention to quality.

300S and Sc, Coupe, Cabriolet and Roadster. Movie stars like Bing Crosby and Clark Gable were quick to snap up the sporty 300S two-door model. In concept it was a modern 540K. Only 560 units were made. A rare Sc model (fuel-injected) was also built — only 200 units. The S and S came as fixed Coupes, Cabriolets with irons and folded top visible, and as Roadsters without landau-irons and the top hidden when folded. The S was produced between 1951 and 1955, the Sc between 1955 and 1958. The latter is now the most sought-after of all postwar Mercedes models.

300SL Coupe and Roadster. A classic from introduction, the production 300SL was an outgrowth of the all-conquering competition 300SLs. The gullwing doors of the Coupe were a necessary novelty due to the space frame chassis. Only 1,400 units were made between 1954 and 1957. The Roadster (with reworked space frame and conventional doors) sold 1,858 units from 1957 to 1963. The Coupe, with its gullwing doors, reached a higher visibility than any other Mercedes, and with that came instant collectability. The Roadster, after a slower start, is now close behind.

190SL Roadster. A junior 300SL, based on the 180 Sedan, was for the affable, less racing-interested clientele. Only 120hp, but high in quality, production was 25,881 units, showing that the concept of a comfortable, less-powerful touring car was a winner. For a long time a relative sleeper, the 190SL is now gaining popularity as a collector Mercedes in its own right. It was produced between 1955 and 1963.

220S and 220SE Coupe and Cabriolet. The styling of this model was not far removed from the earlier 220, but the slab side was new. A grace of line, regal perhaps, typified these cars. Only 3,429 220S units were made from 1956 to 1959. The 220SE, which had fuel injection, was made between 1958 and 1960. Production was 1,942 units. This model was always appreciated by the enthusiast. It possessed the timeless lines that made it look expensive and elegant long after production had ended.

220SEb Coupe and Cabriolet. This is a modern classic. Unlike the 220SEb Sedan, the Coupe and Cabriolet did not have fins. Simple lines, beautiful and

In 1952, racing fans were stunned by the revelation of a new Mercedes sports racing car. Entered in Italy's Mille Miglia, it took second place. Left top, the coupes parade through the streets of Brescia. Entered in Switzerland's Bremgarten, they took a triple victory. Fritz Reiss is seen to the right. In France's Le Mans, the 300SL's took first and second. Norbert Niedermeyer, captured at speed, to the lower left. In Germany's Nürburgring, a row of four roadsters crossed the finish line. Reiss shows his style above. Added to these successes was a victory in Mexico's Carrera Panamericana. A fantastic record year – setting the stage for Mercedes' magnificent postwar comeback.

restrained, made it an enduring favorite. Introduced in 1960, 16,902 units had been sold when production ended in 1965. This model is still relatively affordable, but available examples may require restoration too costly to be justified by their present value.

300SE Coupe and Cabriolet. Basically, this model has the same look as the 220SEb, but with the larger engine, air suspension and four-wheel disc brakes, it is a more advanced piece of engineering. In this case, because of the unique suspension, the Sedan may also be considered collectable. Production figures for the Sedans: 6,848 units; for the Coupe and Cabriolet: 3,127 units. In 1965, a new body appeared on the Sedan. Another 5,106 units were made of this model. the same rule of collectability is valid for the 300SE as for the 220 SEb, except that with the more complicated suspension, and maintenance, it will be even more expensive to restore.

230SL, 250SL, 280SL Roadster. This is the model that replaced the 190SL. Personal transportation in sumptuous elegance was still the theme. This car is timeless in its classic simplicity. Introduced in 1963, it went through two displacement increases and was built until 1971. Production numbers were: 230SL 19,831; 250SL 5,196, and 280SL 23,885, for a total of 48,912 units. The cars came with four-speed automatic or manual, or five-speed optional. Many units were produced, but not enough to meet the demand. A sound and enjoyable investment.

600 Limousine and Pullman. This automobile brought back the term "Grosser Mercedes" or "Grand Mercedes," recollecting the 7.7-liter Limousines of the late thirties. The Limousine and the stretched Pullman versions are both magnificent automobiles, conceived for executives and heads of state. Introduced in 1963, only a total of 1,960 Limousines and 364 Pullmans had been produced by 1973. The last 600 is believed to have been completed in 1981. Prices for examples in prime condition stay high. The 600 is looked upon as the finest automobile of its type ever built.

250SE and 280SE Coupe and Cabriolet. More power is found in both cars, as compared to the 220SEb, but virtually identical looks. Production of the 250SE Coupe and Cabriolet was 6,213 units; of the 280SE 5,187, from 1965 to 1972. Conventional suspension makes these models less expensive to restore and maintain. Also, examples of later years can still be found in excellent original condition.

300SEL 6.3 Sedan. The connoisseur's muscle car was available only as a sedan. What a shame. As such, it will probably not hit the stride that a two-door

With the publicity generated by the racing victories, came a need for new products. New generations of bread-and-butter cars were soon introduced and the facilities took on a more automated look, top left. The 180-line was first shown in 1953, its diesel version seen to the right. The following year a more luxurious range, the 220-series, left, was introduced. The 190SL, above, built between 1955 and 1963, hardly seems to qualify as a bread-and-butter model; but conceived to capitalize on the success of the 300SL, this small brother did the trick, with more than 25,000 units produced.

model would have. But with a production of only 6,526 units from 1967 to 1972, it could do better than expected. Maybe it is a sleeping giant. Two facts are clear, however: It is the most desirable of the Mercedes sedan, and still the fastest sedan on the road.

250C and 280C Coupe. These sporty little hardtops still had the six-cylinder motor. They had the same wheelbase and overall length as the 250 Sedan, but looked somewhat better. Relatively high prices indicate a potential sleeper. Production figures: 250C 42,290, 280ZC 23,576. About half were fuel-injected, but these were not sold in the United States. Made from 1968 to 1975.

280SE 3.5 Coupe and Cabriolet. This model has the same body style as the 220SEb, originating way back in 1960, but comes with the 3.5-liter V-8. A lower and wider grille was used. It was also faster. Only 4,502 units were made between 1969 and 1971. This is the ultimate Mercedes four-seat coupe and convertible. As such, the convertible holds the position as the third most desirable of the postwar Mercedes models, surpassed only by the 300S and SC, and the 300SL Coupe and Roadster.

350SL and 450SL Roadster. The replacement for the 280SL was the 350SL, first shown in 1971. Even though it was a totally new design, it did carry on the family resemblance, but now it was bigger and heavier, and also looked it. In Europe, the 350SL actually had a 3.5-liter engine. In the United States it had a 4.5-liter power source right from the beginning, but was still labeled 350SL. From 1973 on, it was correctly called 450SL.

Between 1971 and 1973, 11,230 350SLs and 18,258 450SLs were built. An attractive feature of this model was that it always came with both the soft and hard top. The 450SL still has a few years to go before it will be replaced. As always, collectability increases when production stops. Of the U.S. version, the early years, with the small bumpers and the hubcapped wheels, are most desirable to the collector.

350SLC and 450SLC Coupe. The Coupe was fourteen inches longer than the Roadster counterpart. It had a rear quarter window with decorative vertical louvers and a real back seat that could carry two more passengers. It had the same engine as the Roadster, and was also introduced the same year, 1971. There were 9,318 350SLCs made between 1971 and 1973 and 6,294 450SLCs were made in 1972 and 1973. From a collector's viewpoint, the Roadster is the more desirable of the two, mainly because of its sportier looks and open-air option.

220A CABRIOLET

Sugar Cane, Palms and Other Exotic Species...

There was almost total stillness inside the narrow valley between the hills.

Above the valley, moving like gigantic cotton floats, were woolly-white clouds. They moved very slowly. And when they passed in front of the sun, the huge dark shadows they made drifted, also very slowly, across the fields of tall ripening sugar cane that covered the valley floor.

Above the floor, if you looked closely, you could see that there was a breeze. It moved up there among the palm crowns. The palms grew towering and tall-trunked in long, arrow-straight columns that lined the sides of the narrow roads crisscrossing the Santa Teresa plantation. The breeze stroked the long branches very gently, making them shiver just enough so you could see it.

But there was no breeze near the ground. Only the hot air moved, vibrating with heat as it rose from the burning soil. Every time there was a shadow the vibration stopped and it was gone as long as that merciless sun was gone.

It was siesta time on the plantation.

José Harth, owner of the 1953 Mercedes-Benz 220A Cabriolet parked in the middle of the road, lounged beside it on the grass, his head and shoulders propped up against one of those wide-bellied old palm trunks. His eyes were closed.

Alberto, the Chilean chauffeur, sat in the shade underneath the open hatch of the Wagoneer. He sipped

(continued on overleaf)

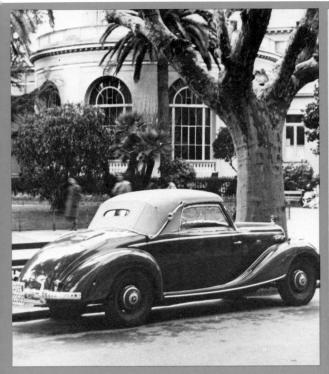

The 170V, left, was produced in ninety thousand examples between 1936 and 1942. When production was re-started after the war, in 1946, this model again became the bread-and-butter line. It had a four-cylinder engine that produced thirty-six hp. Top speed was sixty-two mph. Early production consisted mainly of utility vehicles, such as delivery vans and ambulances. The model remained in production until 1953. Its most successful year was 1951, when almost thirteen thousand units were made. Already, in 1949 came improved versions with stronger engines, better weight distribution and smoother styling of the hood. From a collector's viewpoint, the Cabriolets are the most desirable. Above, a 170S Cabriolet A, the two-seat version, parked on a street in Cannes, France. To the upper right, an offical factory photo of the same model. Note the separate, fully chromed headlights. To the right, the 170S Cabriolet B, the four-seat version.

Palms, planted almost two hundred years ago, line the narrow roads cutting through the Santa Teresa sugar plantation, east of Caracas, Venezuela. The 220A Cabriolet stands out like a magnificent sculpture of steel and leather. The tall radiator, the narrow hood, the swooping fenders, all reflect its prewar heritage. Jose Harth obtained his Survivor, chassis number 187.012.031.32/53, in 1975 from a doctor who had owned it since new. Built in 1953 – one of 403 convertibles produced that year – it still has only 87,000 kilometers on the odometer.

from a bottle of Coke while his eyes wandered across the hillsides, looking for nothing in particular.

I had just put away my camera; it seemed like a crime against local custom to work in the middle of the day. I walked over to the silver Mercedes sitting there like a shining sculpture of steel and leather.

Now, thirty years after it had been built, the car still looked very beautiful, maybe more so, I thought to myself as I slid in behind the big white three-spoked steering wheel. The door opened suicide-style, making entry easy.

The leather that covered the seats, door panels and dashboard was still bright red, except where sun and wear had faded and polished it. The wood was perfect. The radio in its wooden console was still the original one.

The two knobs on each side of the ashtray located on top of the dash — the left controlling the windshield wipers, the right containing the cigarette lighter — and the knobs governing the ignition setting, the headlights, the instrument lights and the choke — all located on the lower edge of the dashboard — were all chromed. So were the levers controlling the heating and ventilation settings, the airflow nozzles, the door handles and the window cranks — all chromed, so that they all matched.

Everything you could see was made from basic, honest material — leather, wood, steel, glass, rubber — all, except the steering wheel. It was made from some kind of plastic that looked like ebony. The small knob on the end of the column-mounted shift lever was apparently made from a different kind of plastic — it had turned yellow.

There were two large gauges on the dashboard, one on each side of the steering column — a clock to the left, a speedometer to the right. The odometer showed 87,000 kilometers. Original mileage, José had told me.

He had bought the 220 from its first owner, a doctor, and had himself put only about ten thousand kilometers on it during the past seven years.

Today's trip would be the longest, he had said.

We had started early in the morning from José's home built right on top of the highest ridge of the mountain to the south of Caracas. The undersides of the clouds had brushed the roof of the house and, sitting there on the veranda, it had felt like sitting in an airplane coming in for a landing, the city sprawling long and narrow in the valley below, white in that mild forgiving morning sunlight, blue mountain ranges on all sides, the mass of office skyscrapers and apartment highrises looking like vertical brush strokes in an impressionist painting, the brick-red shantytowns showing vaguely on

the hillsides to the east and west, the Atlantic shimmering brightly through an opening in a mountain chain.

In back of the house, inside a high wall, behind a gate, under protecting roofs, stood two rows of the most desirable postwar Mercedes collector cars you could assemble — a 300SL Gullwing, a 300SL Roadster, a 300Sc Coupe, a 300Sc Roadster, just to mention a few.

José Harth was foremost among a handful of super-enthusiasts in Venezuela. He had begun cultivating his interest in cars many years ago — while his friends were still laughing at his eccentric passion. He had searched towns and villages for cars as he traveled the country in his business. He had become familiar with nearly every old car in existence. He knew their whereabouts, their conditions, their owners — and what it would take to obtain them.

José had told me all this with great excitement, as if it had pleased him much to finally meet another enthusiast just as car crazy as himself.

He had met me at the plane arriving from San Juan at midnight. Driving back, it had taken more than an hour to get up the hill — traffic had been heavy in spite of the late hour. When we arrived at his home, the rows of those beautiful cars had become another obstacle — enjoyable, of course. Then there had been more talk in the library — between sips of French cognac so fine we never got a headache, between cooling breezes from windows open to city lights far below, between music from sapitos — those tiny frogs that sound like they carry their own little marimba, constantly hitting the same high note. We had been up till three in the morning. That was only a few hours ago, I thought to myself, sliding a little deeper into the comfortable seat. I had driven the 220 up from Caracas. We had passed through the city on the freeway that runs the length of it, then continued on a highway to the southeast, passing through thick-foliaged forests and green fields.

Driving the 220, I realized it was indeed a postwar link with the prewar past. The steering, the controls, the handling — all reminded me of classics I had driven. Even the view from the driver's seat was classic — the flat dash that narrowed, like on a boat; the long, slim, tall hood with the star way out there; the swooping fenders...

I felt myself slide farther down. Comfortable, I thought to myself. Those Mercedes designers sure knew how to make a car comfortable. I let my neck rest against the top of the seatback and reached up to adjust the visor so the sun would not shine in my eyes. Comfortable, I repeated...

It was siesta time on the plantation.

The 220 model appeared in 1951. It was a vastly improved vehicle, now sporting a new six-cylinder engine that developed eighty hp. Top speed was about ninety mph. The model carried on the basic styling theme of the 170, but was now larger and roomier, and also had a much more luxuriously appointed interior. The headlights were mounted inside the fenders instead of outside, as on the 170. To the left, a 220 Sedan captured against the background of Monte Carlo. Above, a 220 Cabriolet B on tour through the Schwarz-wald region in Germany. To the right, for both the 170 and the 220, fitted luggage was an option, so that, if so desired, the trunk space could be utilized to its maximum.

300Sc ROADSTER

Up That Last Long Hill to Caracas...

The road snaked through the jungle like a narrow river. Here and there the jungle opened up and you could see traces of man; fields had been cleared long ago and bamboo planted around them. The bamboo grew thick and impenetrable now, like the jungle itself.

The Mercedes rolled like a boat in heavy seas as it charged ahead. Two cones of spinning dust came shooting out from behind the rear wheels and united farther back into a cloud that continued to twist and swirl until the turbulence went out of it, leaving the dust to sink slowly into the foliage. The ice chest with the beer and soda inside, the short wooden step ladder and my aluminum camera cases were making noises as they slid around on the fold-down seat behind us.

José Harth, owner of the 1957 300Sc Roadster, was at the wheel. I was in the passenger seat. He had driven very slowly going the other way earlier. But then it was important to keep the car clean for the pictures. Now we were in a hurry to get back to Caracas before the sunlight would be gone.

Between potholes and curves I was thinking about the location we had just left. It was a stroke of luck to have found it; like finding the needle in a haystack. I had described to José what I saw in the back of my mind. He had a vague mental picture of having seen such a place: Hacienda Iscaragua, built in 1837. It said so, right above the gate. A ruin now, coffee beans had once covered the slopes. When the profit went out of lowland-grown coffee the hacienda had been abandoned and the buildings left to deteriorate.

I was lucky, too, that I was dealing with an owner like
(continued on overleaf)

The 300S and Sc models were handbuilt automobiles, even though these photographs from the
factory give an impression of assembly line pro-
cedures. Of course, it is all in the speed with which
the line moves! Judging from the number of cars
in presence, the photographs were probably taken
during the latter part of 1952, just after production had reached a serious pace. At that time
the average production was one car a day.
Later, in 1954, 1955 and 1957, production averaged
barely one car per week! The photographs show
the stage where body panels were checked for final
fit. As can be seen, the lowly file was still an important tool then.

Styling, craftsmanship and performance of this 300Sc Roadster brought back the glory-days of prewar 500K and 540K Roadsters. It is remarkable that Mercedes was again able to create an automobile that rivaled what had already become the standard of excellence. The fuel-injected Sc even outperformed its prewar counterparts. This beautiful 1957 Survivor, chassis number 180015-7500021 – all original except for the paint – was photographed in Caracas, Venezuela. In 1978, Jose Harth was finally able to obtain it from its second owner, an airline pilot, after having been on its trail for several years.

José, I thought to myself. Altogether, there were fewer than two hundred of these cars, the most valuable of all postwar Mercedes models. What were the odds in favor of finding an owner with José's philosophy? An owner who was willing to drive wherever the best location took him? Willing to take the risk a great photograph often requires?

We even had to build a primitive ramp of bricks and dirt to get the car into the courtyard. Where the mossy old tiles were. Where the pillars were. And the white-washed walls with the layers of old paint showing through here and there. Lavender.

It had been tough going getting in there.

Don't worry, José had said, when I looked sick from hearing the frame scrape against the bricks. Don't worry! This car is built like a railroad car. It was meant to be driven hard. This car you can't kill driving. It was built like a tank. Not like a railroad car. Like a tank! Sí, Señor! It should be driven. That's what it was built for. For what else would you use the car? You can't let it sit around. That's what makes it go bad!

I liked his philosophy.

Not that he was careless. Far from it. He kept all his cars in top shape. Not in concourse shape; but clean. Working properly. And he was fanatical about authenticity. A car was always better when it was used. The patina gave the car charm. Like a walked-in pair of shoes. Of course, there had to come a day when restoration was necessary. But that day should be postponed as long as possible.

I hope it was all worth it, I thought to myself as we came to the end of the dirt road. If the picture came out as good as it looked in the viewfinder, it would be worth it. Maybe a cover shot, I thought. But it should really have had everything in it. The stream on the other side of the main building. The jungle rising beyond it. And the parrots.

José wanted me to drive now. I slid in behind the wheel, found first gear, and accelerated out onto the paved road. There was that column-mounted shift lever again, same as on the 220. I just couldn't get used to it. It was as if I was stirring a pot of oatmeal. And then there was the gigantic steering wheel. Also a little hard to get used to. Especially since it required great movements to keep in touch with the direction of the wheels. I was moving my arms like you would when making fun of an old lady in her '52 Olds.

But those were unimportant observations. The overpowering fact was that almost no other car in the world could have given me the feeling of flying high as did this magnificent machine. I'm not talking about putting on

The 300S and Sc models were available in three different body styles: the Cabriolet, pictured above, which had the decorative landau irons and a roof that folded down in the traditional fashion, leaving it protruding from the rear deck; the Coupe, above right, which had a steel top that could not be removed; the Roadster — the last of the cars lined up in the picture to the lower right — which was equipped with a top that disappeared completely behind the seats, allowing for an uninterrupted rear deck line. The car pictured in the background is a 300 Cabriolet B. To the left, the instrument panel of the 300S.

the helmet and the driving suit. I'm talking about sliding into a tuxedo on a Monday morning!

After a few minutes on the paved road we reached the three-lane highway between Caracas and Guarenas. José told me to turn left. I accelerated through the gears with the engine purring quietly. Only at the end of each gear, when I kept the pedal down a little longer, letting the revolutions come rolling, did the engine give off an excited snarl. The wind was flowing briskly across the open cockpit now, grabbing our clothes, pulling our hair. The air was warm, and smooth as silk. I figured the sun had about five more minutes to go. Ahead, there was a long sweeping turn before the highway began to rise slowly, turning uphill, rising for ten or fifteen miles, leading to a summit and a final approach to the city.

José suddenly turned to me, shouting, "This is my favorite time of the day. I wanted to hurry back so you could have the pleasure of driving up this hill with the sun going down."

I smiled a thank you without taking my eyes off the road. We were doing about ninety kilometers an hour. In fouth. I shouted back to José, "Does it beat the 540K?"

"Sí, Señor! Claro!"

"Let's compare. The 540 had a straight-eight. Right? Pushrod. One hundred eighty horses!"

"But remember, that was with the supercharger going. This one has a straight-six. Overhead cam. One hundred seventy-five horses! And it's two thousand pounds lighter! You know what that means."

"Okay. But the frame is about the same, isn't it? Suspension too. Swing-axle. Right?"

"Yes, but this one has the single-pivot axle. Like on the 300SL Roadster. Handles better. And it has fuel injection. What was the top speed of the 540K?"

"One hundred sixty."

"Give it full throttle, Henry!"

I downshifted to third and pushed the pedal to the floor. The car surged. The speedometer needle swung to one hundred twenty. I shifted to fourth when the snarl got angry. The car continued to surge, passing new cars with expressionless look-what-I-am-driving types behind the wheel, passing old cars with neck-turning, surprise-faced passengers, passing over-crowded buses with lots of faces, a look-at-that-old-car expression on them, the owners of the faces hanging out through the open windows, smiling, waving, shouting, all while the old workhorses spewed out clouds of exhaust, laboring hard in low gear.

I looked at the needle again — one hundred sixty.

"It's doing it uphill!"

"Sí, Señor!"

300SL COUPE

By the Grand Piano, a Gullwing!

"The Gullwing!"

Even before Alex Dearborn answered I knew I had asked an unnecessary question. How could a man who had built a business and a lifestyle around a single automobile — who even kept an example of it in his living room — be expected to say anything else?

We sat quietly, both looking at the silver Gullwing parked over by the grand piano. It was placed there like an art object. Which it was!

No ordinary car, the Gullwing, I thought. And Alex, no ordinary man — no ordinary living room!

The home of Alex Dearborn was the former carriage house of a large estate located one-half-hour's drive northeast of Boston. It had been built by a railroad tycoon in the early part of this century. Some years ago the land and the various buildings on it had been split into smaller parcels. The carriage house itself was grand enough for a king.

Alex and his family occupied the upstairs portion. One end of it alone was so roomy the kids used it for a basketball court. Downstairs, in the middle of the facade, were the entrance doors, themselves magnificent examples of old-time craftmanship. Inside, to the right, were the stables. But, where horses used to be kept, now stood rows of Mercedes collector cars. To the left, with floor and walls and ceiling covered by Southern pine, was the hall where the carriages used to stand — now the living room!

It was a huge room, more like a grand ballroom, with high ceilings and an enormous fireplace. In the old days it was where hunting parties gathered before and after the day's activities. Now there were oriental rugs, plush sofas, comfortable chairs, coffee tables, antique lamps and large desks — stacked high with automotive literature.

Alex had a fire going. The light from the flames

Above top, the very first version of the 300SL. Note that the gullwing doors have not yet been cut down into the side panels. Left, the design of the space frame was arrived at through experiments with models. Above, the engine compartment of the racing version. Opposite page, top, Rudolf Uhlenhaut, responsible for the technical development of the 300SL, photographed beside the chassis. This picture clearly shows the angle of the engine. To the left, the interior of the open cars raced at the Nürburgring. To the right, the interior of the car displayed at the New York Auto Show in 1954. Bottom right, the first prototype of the production version 300SL. Note the different treatments of nose and hood.

flickered, making patterns that danced on the paneling and colored and warmed our faces. His looked like that of an English gentleman, fair-skinned and honest-eyed, with features that had been molded by a stubborn strength.

We were waiting for the other guests to arrive; Alex had invited a few car-enthusiast friends for an informal get-together.

"The Gullwing was always your favorite?"

"Yes, as long as I can remember. But to begin with I didn't know enough about Mercedes cars to know about the Gullwing, from a technical viewpoint, I mean. I had to learn the hard way. The first Mercedes I owned was a 1954 220 Sedan. Still have it, matter of fact! Bought it for six hundred dollars. It needed a lot of work. Trouble was I couldn't find anyone competent to do it! That's how I discovered there was a need. So, I decided to open a shop. But I would specialize in Mercedes cars from the fifties. No other models! No other marques! That was in 1972."

"It obviously worked very well!"

"Very well indeed!"

"And now you've sold that business?"

"Yes, in 1978 I sold it to my employees, headed by Paul Russell. The Gullwing Service Company they call it. My own business is still named Dearborn Automobile Company. You see, I was faced with a dilemma! I got more and more involved with the brokerage of cars. It was finally too much to handle both businesses. Besides, I saw an opportunity to realize an idea I'd had for some time. So I bought a larger building in Topsfield. The original business was moved from Marblehead to the new facility. There we had room for an additional four businesses, all catering to Mercedes cars — but all independently owned and operated! You see the advantages? I also formed a new company, specializing in the leasing of old and new Mercedes cars. It's called Boston Leasing Company. So now we have — all under one roof — a service shop for newer models, a body shop for older models, a body shop for newer models, the original restoration shop, and my showroom..."

There were sounds from cars driving up in front of the house. Alex left to greet the guests. I was too exhausted from two days of photographing the Gullwing to even attempt to get up from the deep of the sofa. I let my eyes return to the bulky, bulbous, brutish-bold shapes of the Gullwing, standing there in the room, big-wheeled and beautiful.

Everything about the car is extraordinary, I thought to myself. Just to sit inside that cockpit is extraordinary, the (continued on overleaf)

One of the most talked-about automotive designs of all time, the 300SL Gullwing hardly needs an introduction. This 1955 Survivor, chassis number 198040-550042, belongs to Alex Dearborn of Topsfield, Massachusetts, who has received international recognition for the fine Mercedes automobiles he restores and purveys. A remarkable quality of this track-proven sports racing car is that it not only looks awesome but also elegant, as evidenced by these photographs, taken in front of the carriage house Dearborn has converted to garage his inventory as well as his personal collection.

seat grabbing a hold of you so firm, the ledge and the tunnel surrounding you so protectively, those two big gauges staring back at you so invitingly, the doors curving above you so curiously, their chromed telescope tubes shining brightly. Even entering the car is extraordinary, I thought, the way you have to do it just right: treading one leg in first, placing the foot far back on the floor board, then sitting down on the leather-covered ledge, then leaning in at the same time as you grab hold of the tunnel — placing your hand far enough back so as not to lose your balance when you let yourself drop into the seat — then following with the other leg, bending the knee, grabbing the ankle with the left hand, pulling the doubled-up leg back toward you while you sweep it over and across that ledge — not hitting leather!

You could tell from scratch marks whether owners had bothered to learn the technique or not.

And, of course, driving it was extraordinary, I thought to myself: pulling the choke, turning the key, the gauges coming to life; then pushing the start button while pressing the pedal lightly, the engine coming to life, a little unsure of itself, clearing its throat, then straightening up when you patted the pedal a few times; the engine rumbling sound and deep-voiced, then taking off with that whining sound from the transmission; accelerating out onto the open road; listening to that open-mounted hissing from the engine sucking in air when you floored the pedal; going through the gears; and when you let up between shifting, listening to that sound from behind you, sounding a little like when you were a boy and you ran along a picket fence with your stick . . .

Yes, the Gullwing was extraordinary all around. A race car for the road! Was Ferrari first with that concept? I asked myself. No, of course not, the world's oldest car company had done it before, in the twenties, I remembered, with its SS model.

The Gullwing had to be counted among the three top postwar sports cars, I decided. What about the other two? The Ferrari GTO was worthy. And a Jaguar? The XK120? Too many made? The XKSS? Too few made?

The guests were introduced. Terry Bennett. Paul Russell. Christopher Smallhorn.

"Name the three most outstanding sports cars of the early postwar period."

It was a challenge that caused enough thought and discussion to outlast the evening. To outlast Alex's supply of fire wood. As well as his Dubonnet.

There was of course no agreement. We were all of different temperament. But one car kept cropping up!

How could it not? Especially with one sitting right there in the living room!

Featured on these pages is a unique series of photographs from the factory, showing various steps during the assembly of the 300SL. To the far left, the jig is used to check the form of the body panels. Top left and above, it took a lot of skill to make the gullwing doors fit perfectly. Note the lighter color of the hood, together with the doors and the trunk lid, made from aluminum. To the near left, the engine is lowered into the chassis. The fuel injection side is toward the front. To the right, the body, with all its panels fitted, but still lacking paint and interior trim, is mated with the chassis, lacking only wheels.

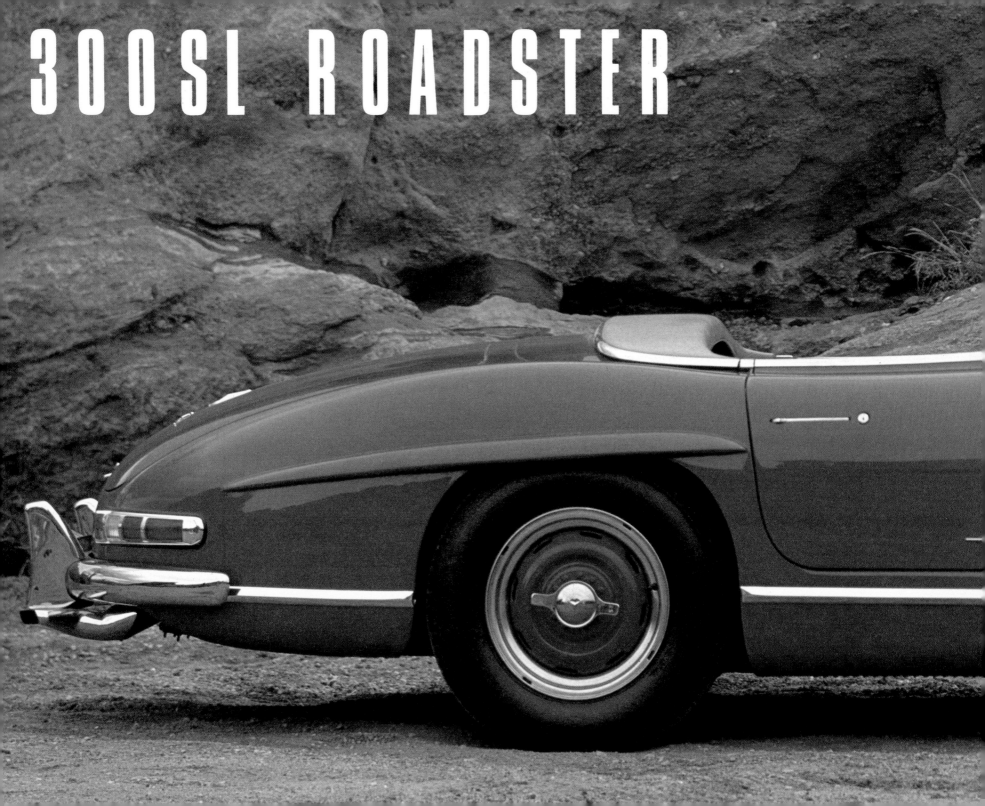

300SL ROADSTER

Promising Beginning, Regrettable Ending.

When you make your living photographing cars, as I do, you spend a lot of time thinking about the sky and what you see up there. Where is the sun coming up? Going down? Is it going to shine at all or is it going to be overcast?

On the day I had arranged to take pictures of Manfredo Lippmann's 1958 300SL Roadster the weather report had promised partly cloudy skies with a chance of rain in the late afternoon. Especially in the foothills. Snow in the mountains.

The location I had chosen, Red Rocks, west of Denver, was located in the foothills. Rain isn't welcome when you take pictures of an open car. But it was still my number one choice; the rough red rocks would look very dramatic behind the smooth red roadster.

I had spent the morning making a final check of the location. The sky was good, a haze covering the sun cast an even light on the formations. The Rockies rose blue and fuzzy-peaked in the distance.

When I arrived at the warehouse where the 300SL was stored, it turned out that the caretaker had no time to come along; my chaperone had more important things to do. It meant I could have the 300SL all to myself. You always have a better time without a chaperone, I thought to myself as I took off.

Driving it along the backroads up into the foothills, I had a strong sensation of doing something I had done before. I couldn't remember where or when. Only that there was something uncomfortable connected with the experience.

But it felt good to be back behind the wheel. It was good to feel that fifties feeling again; that big and heavy feel of the steering wheel, feeling the suspension kick-

Captured at speed on the Nürburgring, above, is the open version 300SL sports racing car. Driven by Fritz Reiss, it came in third in a victorious row of four such cars. To the left, Rudolf Uhlenhaut, in charge of racing development — as competent behind the wheel as any of the competition drivers — gets ready for the first test in the open version 1955 300SLR. Two years later came the open version 300SL — one could have wished for a development of the SLR, rather than a refinement of the SL. Opposite page, American Paul O'Shea, seen at Bridgehampton, successfully campaigned a factory-prepared Roadster during the 1957 season, capturing the SCCA title.

ing you innocently in the seat, that typical 300SL feeling, rather trucklike — less so in the Roadster, but still there.

When I arrived at the location, the sky had changed. There were big clouds up there so that part of the time the sun was bright, making dark definite shadows, and part of the time obscured, making weak fuzzy-edged shadows.

I preferred to shoot when the sun was gone. It meant I had to wait for long periods. While I sat there, my back against a rock, looking at the sensous shapes of the Roadster, I felt that strange sensation again. The disappointment too.

It was a pity the Roadster turned out to be the last true Mercedes sports car, I thought to myself. There should always have been a high-performance machine in the model line-up!

The excitement began with the original 300SL, that first racing version running away from its competition in 1952. It had the innovative space frame that made it so light. And it had those round, smooth shapes that allowed it to shoot through the air like a bullet. The first version had the gullwing doors end at the bottom edge of the windows. The next version got the doors cut down a ways into the body side panels. There was also a Roadster version. Altogether only ten cars were made. Then there was the pre-production version — only one made — with slightly different front-end styling. Next came the production Gullwing, fourteen hundred made, and finally the Roadster, about eighteen hundred.

The Roadster differed from the Gullwing in more ways than it first appears to, I thought to myself. They didn't just cut the roof off. The front and rear ends were made one inch longer, adding two inches to the overall length. The rear fender was made higher, the trunk more drawn out, the splash shields above the wheels longer, the chrome strips coming out from the side vents also longer. And, of course, the headlights were now vertical with smoothly shaped glass covers. And then there was the wraparound windshield.

But it was really under the skin that it differed the most. That original racing car had three downdraft Solex carbs. The output was 175 hp. Top speed about 150 mph. The weight was less than 2,000 pounds. On the production car the carbs had been replaced by fuel injection. The output was now 215 hp, but the weight had increased by almost 1,000 pounds! Top speed was about 140 mph. The frame was the same as on the racing version. So was the suspension and the wheelbase. But front and rear tracks were almost four inches narrower on the Gullwing.

(continued on overleaf)

Decoratively pitched against the rough shapes created by the Hands of Nature are the smooth forms made by the Hands of Man; dramatic cliff formations in Red Rocks National Park, west of Denver, Colorado, is the setting for these photographs of Manfredo Lippmann's 1958 300SL Roadster, chassis number 198042-8500126. A recent restoration has returned it to the same condition it was in when Lippmann took delivery of it brand new. The unique knock-off wheels are still there – a reminder of the days long ago when he piloted the 300SL over tough road racing courses all across Central America.

The Gullwing had two major flaws: handling and brakes. And two major drawbacks: lack of adequate ventilation and lack of adequate luggage space. The Roadster was an improvement in all areas. It had the new single-pivot swing axle. In 1961 it also got four-wheel disc brakes.

The frame of the Roadster was basically still the same — but now more compact across the side-members. The engine and transmission sat slightly lower in the frame. The front and rear tracks had increased slightly. The fuel tank was smaller, the spare wheel relocated and the trunk, therefore, larger. The ride was a little softer and the steering less direct — the Gullwing took two turns to lock, the Roadster, three.

Unfortunatly, engine output was left unchanged. Unfortunately, because the car had become almost four hundred pounds heavier. So the Roadster actually had a little lower top speed than the Gullwing. It was a deliberate move, I thought to myself. It was a continuation of the concept of "the Mercedes luxury sports car," first applied to the 190SL.

Why didn't they go the other way, I asked myself? They already had the engine and the styling available in the 1955 300SLR. A straight-eight developing 300 hp. Top speed 175 mph! And the styling! That drawn-out nose with headlight covers á la Ferrari Testa Rossa. Only two made of the one with the gullwing doors. As far as I'm concerned a car never had to look any better, I thought.

It looked like there would be no more shooting that day. The clouds had suddenly become thick and unpenetrable. The Rockies were dark gray and washed blurry, like on a watercolor painting. It was snowing up there. That meant it would soon rain down here. I had better get out.

I stood up to collect my camera gear. And just at that moment I suddenly remembered: It was in 1969, in Sweden. I had been looking at a 300SL Roadster to buy. Twenty thousand Swedish crowns; five thousand dollars then. The owner let me have it for the day to try it. I had taken it out in the country, parked it beside the road, against some granite rock formations. Then I had sat down in the grass to look at it. Yes, I remembered now. Later I had driven back on the motorway to Stockholm. I had been doing 225 kmph. Suddenly there had been a ripping sound coming from behind me. I was scared to death and didn't dare to turn my head. Not until I had slowed considerably. The sides of the soft top had broken loose and were flapping in the wind like the flaps of an old-timer's leather helmet.

I never bought the Roadster. It was that feeling of disappointment I still felt inside.

If the Roadster looks longer than the Coupe, as in the picture to the upper right, it must be an illusion — or is it possible that one extra inch up front and one in the back can be seen? The optional hardtop became available late in 1958. The extreme wrap around of the window gave excellent rear vision. In the picture to the lower right, can be seen the vertical headlights and the long chrome strips extending from the sides vents — two of the most obvious styling changes. To the left, the dash of a 1957 prototype. The extremely attractive steering wheel, with its recessed horn button, was unfortunately never placed in production.

190SL ROADSTER

A Scientific Study of Shapes at Sunrise.

It was five in the morning and still pitch dark. A gentle breeze from Cuba came tip-toeing up along the shore. It hardly moved the black branches of the palms that lined Fort Lauderdale's long sandy beach, separating it from the four-lane highway that ran parallel to it.

Lee McDonald and I sat quietly inside his 190SL. The air flowed through the rolled-down windows, feeling crisp but a little nippy from the pre-dawn chill. I felt frozen from having just gotten out of bed. I clenched the white foam-plastic cup with its steaming hot coffee from the all-night coffee shop on the corner of Las Olas and Sunrise Boulevard. Sipping from that cup and warming my hands on it seemed to be the only life-supporting systems in operation.

We were waiting for the sunrise.

Lee was originally from Pennsylvania. He had been a sales manager with the Algar Ferrari dealership before he embarked on a career in auto racing; successful, but cut short from a lack of funds. He had then established Prova, capitalizing on his connections among Ferrari owners, as well as realizing a desire for being his own man and for living where life was pleasant.

Prova specializes in the sales of high-quality collector Ferraris. Right now Lee was trying to find a home for the one-off 250GT Spyder Pinin Farina shown at the Geneva Salon in 1957. It featured a cut-down door on the driver's side and was purchased after the show by Ferrari team-driver Peter Collins. Lee is also working on a film documentary on the life of Enzo Ferrari for Gar-Mac Productions.

Lee had run across the 190SL by accident, at the time not on the lookout for a car, but having always been attracted to its elegant lines. He felt it could be worth-while to try a new set of wheels for cruising around Fort

Lauderdale where the climate certainly favors year-round top-down motoring. The car was also exceptionally well preserved having been pampered since new by its owner Haddon Judson, a prominent name in automotive circles and a manufacturer of superchargers and magnetos. The paint had faded a little over the years, so Lee had Durland Edwards give it a top notch paint job. The car is one of the earliest cars produced, number 240, to emerge in 1955.

Looking out across the waves I became aware of a slight bluing of the sky. It was reflected in the glossy never-still surface of the Atlantic. The surf landed on the beach with a slow, soothing rhythm. But I knew from experience that it would all happen very quickly when it finally did happen. I decided to get my camera in position at once. I had found a portion of the beach where two lone palms leaned their slim bent trunks, making long lazy expressions against the lightening sky. The 190SL stood parked in front of them, carefully positioned so as to counterbalance the weight of the still-black palm crowns.

I had decided to place the Mamyia low, in fact, right on the pavement of the opposite far-left lane. Never in the habit of using a tripod, I folded one of Lee's polishing rags and placed it under the camera so it could be easily angled. Flat on my stomach — Lee watching for early-bird traffic — I checked the viewfinder. It looked good.

All I needed now was a colorful sunrise.

I sat down on the edge of the sidewalk, waiting for it to come, when I suddenly remembered the photographs stowed away in the back of my camera case. I got them out and lit my pen-size flashlight.

"Hey, Lee! Ever seen these? The 190SL prototype," I said. "See that strange nose? Angular. More protruding. And that hood? Opens up all the way down to the grille. There's a hood scoop too! And look at the shape of that rear fender. Flatter on top."

Lee bent down to take a closer look, then straightened to check his own car, sitting there across from us, subtly illuminated by the street lights.

"There's no splash shield above the rear wheel arch on that prototype car!" he said. "See that?"

"Yes. Look at yours. Yours doesn't have any chrome trim on those splash shields and no chrome trim along the bottom edge of the side panel either, below the door. Typical for the early cars! Yours probably didn't come with a hardtop. That option came later and those cars all had the chrome trim."

I shuffled the photographs until I found one of the interior. Lee bent down again.

(continued on overleaf)

The photographs on these pages show the 190SL prototype as it was introduced in 1954. The most obvious differences were found in its styling: slightly more protruding grille; the hood scoop; the hood that opens all the way down to the grille; the shape of the rear fender; the lack of splash panel above the rear wheel. To give the 190SL a more sporty image, a version geared to the weekend racing enthusiast was also made available. It featured low-cut aluminum doors that lacked windows and had a small screen in front of the driver. The idea was that these items could be easily exchanged for the everyday doors and windshield.

arly morning sunlight floats across the waves of the Atlantic, tinting the silver surfaces of Lee McDonald's 1955 190SL Roadster, chassis number 5500230. It is parked beside the main beach in Fort Lauderdale, Florida, where McDonald operates Prova Automotive, an organization specializing in the purveyance of Ferraris and other fine automobiles. The prototype 190SL was first seen in early 1954, but production did not begin until early 1955. Less than 1,800 units were made that year. With its low chassis number, McDonald's is one of the first to emerge from the production line.

"The gauges are arranged differently," he said. "And there's no leather on top of the dash, just a thin strip, padded, it looks like, running all along that upper edge. And look at that bent, long shift lever. Looks like one of those palm trunks!"

"This is the car exhibited at the New York Auto Show early in 1954," I said. "It was featured with one of the first production Gullwings. A curious thing was that both cars had the same rear axle at that time. The old swing axle, you know. But about a year later, when the 190SL production car was introduced, it had the improved low-pivot-point swing axle. Same as on the later 300SL Roadster, but without that big compensating spring. Curious thing is that they kept the old axle on the Gullwing, in spite of the fact that it didn't handle well . . . By the way, the specs for the prototype 190SL called for a column-type shift lever. You could also have the car with a bench seat instead of the buckets!"

I shuffled the photographs.

"Look at this, Lee! You could get cut-down racing doors for it! Aluminum. And a small racing screen, too. The big one came off with two screws. The bumpers came off easily, too. Those were the days of the dual purpose sports car, weren't they!"

"It shows their marketing strategy, too!" Lee said. "Shows that they tried to squeeze as much as possible out of the 190SL looking like the 300SL. There was no way it could have been competitive on the track though! It was way too heavy!"

"Yes, too heavy and too sluggish!" I said. "That racing stuff was only image. It wasn't even needed. The 190SL was a success because of what it was — a classy, comfortable, sporty-looking two-seater!"

I happened to look up at the sky. It had suddenly turned bright yellow to the east. There was a cloud bank sitting heavily on the horizon, hiding the sun that had already risen behind it. The cloud was a dusty pink and had fuzzy orange edges. I knew the picture would change quickly now. Lee and I jumped into action. I laid down flat on the street, looking through the viewfinder. The curved trunks were in there and the crowns, silhouetted black against the sky. And the car was in there, a thin burning outline of orange flowing along its contour.

"Hey, Lee! Turn on the lights!"

It would have to be a time exposure. I pressed down hard on the housing of the Mamyia, holding it perfectly still while I pushed the shutter release.

A moment later the rays of the sun shot across the edge of the cloud and everything became light, all colors consumed now by the brightness of morning.

The 190SL came both as a Roadster and as a Coupe with removable hardtop. Pictured on the opposite page, bottom, is the second version hardtop, introduced in 1959, featuring an enlarged rear window. The 190SL was seldom seen on a racetrack, but here, opposite page, top, the factory has dropped a diesel engine into its smaller sports car for an all-out attack on the world speed record for diesel cars, Class E, under 2000cc. The new record over the standing kilometer was fixed at 98.6 kmph. The seats of the Roadster, above, were inspired by racing buckets. To the right, a Roadster photographed on a picturesque cobblestone street in the German wine-growing community of Pleisweiler.

300d SEDAN

Plain Setting for Fancy Automobile.

The road runs straight like a cutting edge. There are few trees. Fewer houses. Fields, a faded ocher color from the lifeless stubble of last year's crop, extend their planes seemingly all the way to the horizon. Like on an ocean, the curve of the planet is almost there to see.

I am driving a 300d. The engine sounds like it is working too hard, like there should be another gear to engage. I glance at the speedometer. Seventy. When the model got the automatic transmission, an American Borg-Warner unit, it was not well adapted. Jay Pettit, owner of the car, had told me about it earlier. Curiously, the American-market version got a 5.11 rear axle ratio instead of the standard 4.67. It meant lower top speed and higher revs during normal cruising. I slow to fifty and feel the engine settle down to a peaceful hum.

The skyline of Decatur is slowly vanishing behind me as I continue on my way to a location I had found the previous afternoon. The primitive simplicity of the fields would be an effective contrast to the urbane elegance of the 300d. I could visualize the car in front of the ornate entrance to a hotel or the monogrammed awnings of a restaurant. But what would it look like out here? I just hope there will be no unpleasant surprises; like that time in Italy when I had found a place with columns and arches and wild grass in front of them. I had especially liked the grass, growing tall, leaning lazily in the wind. When I came back to photograph the Alfa the next day, the grass had been cut!

The 300d was introduced in 1957. Production began late that year. It was basically a 300 of 1951 vintage, but it now had new styling. The trunk lid and the rear fenders, as well as the front fenders, had been extended, all made possible by a four-inch longer wheelbase. There was also the pillarless window design, a

The photograph above was taken in August of 1957 — before the 300d was officially available. Factory engineers, visible inside the car, are engaged in fine tuning the new automatic transmission. The 300d was even more formal than its predecessor. The rear, left, with its larger trunk and wider window, was an area where obvious changes had been made. Mercedes-Benz, in 1960, presented Pope John with a special 300d — a Landaulet. This version had a convertible top that began just behind the divider window, and a throne-like chair that occupied the entire rear seat. To the right, the Pope gives the car its official blessing.

feature allowing an uninterrupted open window area. The engine, on the original 300 producing one hundred thirty-five horsepower, was now fitted with fuel-injection, which increased power to one hundred eighty horsepower. There was also power steering and, optional from 1959, air conditioning. Jay's example is from 1962, the last year of production, when only forty-five cars were made.

The plains of this part of Illinois are cut up into huge squares separated by the kinds of roads I am driving on. It had been difficult to locate one without power poles and power lines; the poles would destroy the simplicity and the lines would reflect in the polished surface of the car. Where is that road? Have I passed it? I decide to continue straight, searching both sides carefully.

Driving on, I remember something else Jay had told me, something about the power steering. I can feel it. It feels like the assisting impulses are not coordinated with the movements of the steering wheel, causing the car to wander off and you have to correct it. Only the car will then wander off in another direction, so that you have to correct continously. I cannot be sure that it is not a peculiarity to this particular car. Jay seems to think that it might be a characteristic found in all early cars fitted with power assisted steering.

Another element of the 300d that also seems not up to par is the air conditioning. I am not thinking of the way it works — I do not care to try it out, slightly frozen as I am from the pre-spring coolness — but of the way it looks. Two enormous scoops protrude from the rear window deck; they are made from ugly-looking black bakelite and do not at all fit the styling theme of the interior. Below these scoops, inside the trunk, sits the evaporator, taking up a lot of space. It looks a little like the one in my motel room, I think to myself.

Those three elements, the automatic transmission, the power steering and the air conditioning were obviously concessions to American tastes, overtures to an all-out attack on the rich market on the other side of the Atlantic. On subsequent models these elements would be fully developed, but on the 300d they remain curious mementos from an infantile stage.

But there is nothing underdeveloped or immature about the rest of the car, I think to myself as I continue to look for the road. The engineering is built on decades of research and development. The styling is superb. The standard of workmanship is on an exceptionally high level.

It has never been a tradition at Mercedes to give credit to stylists. But they have always touted their

(continued on overleaf)

Representing one of the most prestigious luxury automobiles of its era, this 1962 300d Sedan, chassis number 189.011-12-003131, belonging to Jay Pettit of Decatur, Illinois, retains its majestic elegance even on a narrow farm road, surrounded by freshly plowed fields. In its day the 300d was the means of transportation for dignitaries such as German Chancellor Adenauer as well as President Kennedy on his state visit to Mexico. Pettit, who maintains his beautiful example in perfectly original condition, values it as one of the most outstanding examples of postwar automotive craftsmanship.

engineers. Fritz Nallinger and Rudolf Uhlenhaut, top names during the early postwar period, were always given credit for their innovations. If one searches Mercedes literature with dedication, one will run across the name Karl Wilfert. He was responsible for the styling department during these years. Responsible. Not necessarily the creator of the actual shape! One might also stumble upon the name of Paul Brac, a Frenchman employed at the Mercedes styling department. He was supposedly the man who created the 300SL Gullwing. If this is correct, I think to myself, if he actually did do the 300SL, and if he actually is French, it is ironic that a design always thought of as being typically teutonic, came from the pen of a Frenchman!

I suddenly realize I have forgotten to look for the road. Where is it? Did I pass it? I must have. I decide to turn back.

I remember another subject Jay and I discussed. I had asked him why he was so attracted to the fifties and sixties Mercedes cars. Why that period in particular? The chrome plated brass, he had said. Not the brass itself, of course, but the quality of workmanship and the limited production it symbolized.

The 300d, for instance, he had said, has chrome plated brass stampings and extrusions all over: the windshield and window frames, the radiator, the headlight rims and all the chrome trim. The radiator grid is aluminum. All the die castings are, from necessity, made out of white metal: the star, the door handles, the model identification trim and so on. The bumpers and the hubcaps are pressed steel.

The brass period began to deteriorate with the 280SL, where the side moldings were of aluminum, chemically brightened and anodized — a necessary move to facilitate mass production. But the 280SL is still looked upon as belonging to the brass period.

The 280SL, by the way, is one of Jay's particular favorites. And he should know what he is talking about. A 300Sc Roadster as well as a 300SL Roadster and a 600 Limousine that once belonged to the Shah of Iran are among the other Mercedes cars he owns. Of course, they all have their particular purposes. The 300Sc is the car to use when you go to the club. The 300SL is the car for the track. The 300d is the car to drive to a formal dinner. The 600 is the car in which to pick up business acquaintances. But the 280SL, is the car for the road!

The road! Hey! There it is!

But right where I had planned on placing the car, right there, a tractor was busily plowing the field, destroying it, sending a cloud of dust into the air . . .

In 1951 — after a ten-year respite — Mercedes-Benz was again able to offer a big, impressive, limousine-type automobile. The 300, first shown at the Frankfurt Auto Show, was the embodiment of this theme. The conservative styling, the luxurious interior and the powerful engine, made this model perfectly matched to the demands of such a car. The 300 was most often seen in dark colors, but even in a light color, as in the picture above, it retains its formal elegance. What about when it carries skis on its roof? As in the picture to the left. The photograph to the right, shows the Cabriolet version, of which 642 units were built.

220SE CABRIOLET

The World, According to Mr. Price.

Right beside the Red River, before it joins the mighty Mississippi, right in the heart of Louisiana, there is a city, and in that city there is a big, square, two-story industrial building built from brick, once a Coca-Cola bottling plant, now, without any signs of use, standing there alone in a deteriorating neighborhood. There has been talk about tearing the building down to make room for a new thoroughfare, and if that ever happens Walter Price will have to look for another place to keep his forty Mercedes cars.

Walter Price grew up in that town. And he never left it to live anywhere else. True, he was away while studying architecture at Georgia Tech. And he was gone for a few years during the war. In the Air Force. Navigator on a B-24. After two missions to Anzio (we hit it from the sea . . .), he was shot down over Steyr on his ninth (we took a direct hit in the number two engine and bailed out from twenty-five thousand feet . . .) and was taken prisoner. He was lucky — not all of the men made it (we left two dead in the tail section and one was killed when the plane hit the ground . . .). But except for those detours, (a man has got to learn a profession and he has got to do his duty in wartime . . .), he stayed faithful to the city by the river.

When Walter Price takes you to his building to show you the cars, he will invite you to ride with him in his 1971 280SE Sedan (have had this one since new . . . has got two hundred thousand miles on it now . . .). He will drive *(continued on overleaf)*

Featured on these pages is the work of Kurt Wörner at its best! Almost all the excellent black and white historic photographs in this volume come from his prolific Leica camera, via Road & Track, which purchased the entire collection a few years ago. Wörner chose to capture the essence of the beautiful light-colored 220SE Cabriolet by placing it against the magnificent Swiss Alps, the Brünigpass and the Süstenpass, to be specific. These photographs reflect the pleasure of motoring the way it once used to be — both in Europe and America — when the automobile was not only a means of everyday transportation, but a way to explore the land.

Chromed brass, wood, leather – true materials of the classic automobile – abound in the 220SE Cabriolet. In this perennial favorite, the materials were combined to create one of the most lavishly comfortable models to emerge from Mercedes. The pictures on these pages, photographed on the grounds of a plantation in Louisiana, show the splendor of this 1960 Survivor, chassis number 128.030-10-003042, belonging to Walter Price. The model could not be complemented for speed and power – its attraction lay solely in the areas of styling and comfort – areas in which it could be sure to draw superlatives.

fast, and when you arrive at the building, he will drive right up in front of the tall delivery door, honk three times, and when the door rolls up, rattling and squeaking — seemingly before it has risen high enough to let the car under — he will drive inside, fast. The door will roll down and close behind the car, and, from the outside, everything will look as before — as if the door and the building were never used.

It is dark inside and it will take a while before your eyes are used to it. But soon you will begin to recognize rows of familiar shapes; 220SEb, 250SE, 280SE Sedans and Coupes and Cabriolets, even a few 300SE Coupes and Sedans, sitting there on their knees from the suspensions being shot, all just resting there quietly idle (my brother bought a Mercedes and he told me I ought to get one too . . . he liked it real well, he said . . . I drove his for a week and I couldn't believe what I had missed out on . . . I used to buy a new Lincoln Continental every year . . . no more . . . it was like a religious conversion . . . I had to tell everyone about Mercedes and what a great car it was . . .) Next he will take you past rows of 180 and 220 Sedans in another part of the building, opening hoods and doors on some, wiping a patch of paint clean on others (all this one needs is a new water pump . . . this one has to have the driver's seat replaced . . . see how the paint on this one is still pretty good . . . amazing how well they hold up . . .).

Then he will take you around to the back of the building where engines and axles lay lined up in orderly rows, and hoods and doors and trunk lids stand stacked against the walls, and wrecks sit oily-black and rusty-brown with their guts removed (it got to the point where I thought everyone should drive a Mercedes . . . but I figured not everyone could afford to buy new . . . so I started buying up old ones . . . figured it was my duty to provide people with the best car there was . . . in the end I had six mechanics working for me, full time, just fixing them to sell . . . and I was traveling all over buying every old Mercedes I could lay my hands on . . .).

Then he will take you to another area where there is shelf upon shelf stacked high with trim details, seats, dashes, gauges, steering wheels, wheels, hubcaps (trouble was, the public wasn't ready . . . they were ignorant . . . they were too caught up in this new-model-every-year business . . I've bought and sold about two hundred cars, I figure . . . but I never made any money on them . . . not that that was what I was after . . . but the public just wasn't ready for it . . . have about forty left . . .).

And then there is yet another part of the building, over to the side, the white bottling-plant tiles still covering the

floor. This is the area for the chosen ones — his own collection. There is one 300S Cabriolet, one 300S Coupe, one 600 (this is my second . . . bought my first new in '72 . . . should have never sold it . . .), one 190SL, two 280SL Roadsters, one 280SE 3.5 Cabriolet, one 300SE Coupe, one 280SE Coupe, and several 280SEL and 300SEL Sedans (I'm going to have to thin out among those . . . I'll keep the best one of each . . .).

Just as you think you have seen it all he will take you over to a big elevator. It is big enough to hold a car and . . . yes, you guessed it. He will lower the prison-bar gate, slamming it shut, and the elevator will begin to rise, shivering, shrugging, finally coming to a halt, jerking. Up there it is light and airy. There are wooden floors and antique furniture — the former executive offices. He will bid you to exit the elevator first (after you, sir . . .) and as you round the corner your eyes will be dazzled by an astonishingly well-preserved 300SL Roadster (knew of that one for a long time . . . finally got it last year . . . seven thousand original miles . . .). Beside it stands an almost equally good 300S Cabriolet. And beside it, in the last spot — there is only room for three — an immaculate green 220SE Cabriolet (got a Gullwing under restoration . . . Don't know where to put it . . .).

He will talk at length about the green convertible (this is one of my favorites . . . it's a '60 model . . . they made only twelve hundred that year, handmade . . . it was their top of the line model . . . you could buy the 300 Cabriolet, true, but that was a limo . . . look at all this wood, more wood than in any other Mercedes . . . the new model, the 220SEb, came in '61, was nothing like this . . . this one is the epitome of luxury and craftsmanship . . .). He will invite you to sit behind the wheel and you will understand his enthusiasm, sinking deep into the leather aroma, surrounded by the sight of wood, wood on the dash, burled walnut, four and a half feet of it, solid, so solid it helps stablize the cowl, wood around the windshield, wood on the armrests, leather seats, wide and soft, leather on the door panels, he points (wood, leather, wood, wood . . .).

Now he will turn around and with sweeping gestures tell you what he wants to do up there (I'm going to have car seats set up . . . groups with tables . . . and I'm going to have books and artifacts like a museum . . . and over there I'm going to have a car rotating . . . so you can sit here and look at it from every angle . . .).

Afterward you will know that you have been with a true enthusiast, one of the few who still have an honest regard for what is good and right (those Mercedes cars are built right . . . and I like that . . .).

The 220S and SE came in two luxury versions: Cabriolet and Coupe. The hardtop of the latter was non-removable. The Coupe, pictured above, was even more restrained in its appearance than was the Cabriolet — truly a car for the distinguished lady or gentleman. Its interior, same as that of the Cabriolet, shown to the left, matched the elegance of the exterior. More wood and leather was used than in any other Mercedes of its size. Pictured to the right, the 220S, from which the luxury versions were derived, was also an elegant car. It began life in 1954, and was produced until 1959, at which time more than eighty thousand units had been made.

600 LIMOUSINE

Perfection, for the Sake of Perfection.

I am intrigued to discover yet another oasis, yet another of those refreshing havens of appreciation of quality and craftsmanship that still remains on this desert planet, where sometimes only the crass and the superficial seem to survive.

This particular oasis is flourishing inside an unpretentious gray building in Escondido, a community located twenty miles northeast of San Diego.

Thomas Kreid, a German descendant from Illinois, is the well of this oasis. He would not want to describe himself in those terms, but he is nevertheless, with his two decades of experience, one of the most knowledgeable Mercedes experts around. He has spent the past four years exclusively involved in researching the prewar classics, the 500K and 540K (particular emphasis has been on the Special Roadster, of which one example exists in his collection), and the postwar greats, the 300S and 300Sc, as well as the modern Mercedes giant, the 600.

Inside this oasis I encounter five cars, all in such excellent condition that I have seldom seen a collection like it under one roof.

The first is a metallic-silver 280SL (a restoration exercise, Thomas tells me). After a virtual remanufacture, which took only nine weeks, it was entered in the 1982 National Meet of the Mercedes-Benz Club and was chosen Reserve Best of Show.

The second car is a twelve-thousand-mile 300SL Roadster, probably the best preserved original example in the world. The original whitewalls, Continental Super Record High Speeds, are still on it — not even the weights have been touched! It has unusual color combinations (California colors, Thomas calls them): bamboo interior, ivory exterior, beige hardtop (like coffee with cream, he tells me). This car was the centerfold of

(continued on overleaf)

In spite of all its impressive elegance — as evidenced by the photograph to the left, picturing the 600 Limousine by the shores of Lago Maggiore in northern Italy — there was still an automobile that could top it! That automobile was the bigger brother of the 600 Limousine, the truly majestic 600 Pullman. It was built on a twenty-seven-inch longer wheelbase and was intended for heads of state and other dignitaries. Above, the Pullman, and to the right, the Landaulet (a Pullman with a convertible roof above the rear seat) are pictured during a parade in 1964.

Named the "Grand Mercedes," the 600 Limousine was certainly more grand than anything else Mercedes had ever produced, bringing back memories of the prewar 770K. In the 600, however, classic craftsmanship was combined with modern technology to a degree that had never before been seen – and possibly never again will be. The 1969 600 featured here, chassis number 100.012-12-001481, was photographed in front of San Diego's Del Mar racetrack, and belongs to Thomas Kreid of Carlsbad, California – a connoisseur whose taste for perfection has brought him a reputation as one of the finest restorers around.

the Silver Anniversary issue of *Star*, official publication of the Mercedes-Benz Club.

Third in this lineup is a magnificent burgundy 300Sc Roadster, also restored by Thomas and his team: Stephen Azola, Michael Neuman, Michael Biener, Fidel Gonzales and Axel Jensen. (The skill levels of these men are as high as those of the men who built these cars in the first place, or higher, Thomas feels.) The car won Best of Show at the 1983 Orange County Tribute to Mercedes-Benz, in a field of 130 vehicles.

Another two 300Sc cars, both in the process of being restored, occupy the opposite side of the building. They remind me of a factory scene from the fifties, looking as if they were under assembly there, every component shiny and seemingly new. Rows of shelving, containing a great variety of parts, cover the near end of the building; the far end, is used for painting and for manufacture of fenders and other body panels, formed over jigs made from original patterns.

Next in the lineup come two examples of the 600, one dark blue, the other light metallic-beige, both so exquisitely well preserved they look exactly like they did on the day they were delivered new.

Thomas is called away to the phone, and I sit down behind the wheel of the light-colored car. There is an original British-market sales brochure left on the passenger seat. I pick it up and scan the pages. A headline, "Basic Equipment," catches my eye.

"Lighting: Asymmetrical dipped beam; fog lamps; front and rear limit lights; flashing direction indicators; parking light; reversing light; instrument lights, dimmer-switch controlled; socket for inspection lamp; light in glove box; map-reading light; boot light; foot well lights: two in front, two at rear; roof lights at rear; two adjustable lamps in rear roof pillars.

"Signalling equipment: Headlight flasher; wind horn, and two electric horns; additional high-volume horn available; automatic cancelling of flashing indicators.

"Instruments: Speedometer; rev counter; gear-selector indicator; oil pressure gauge; petrol gauge; engine thermometer; indicator lights for battery charge, flashing indicators, headlight beam, hydraulic system, air pressure, petrol reserve; clock; mileage recorder; trip recorder; outside-air thermometer.

"Locks: Four hydraulically-operated, safety door-locks; central control for locks on doors, boot and petrol-filler cap; manual operation of all door locks from the inside, and of front doors and boot from the outside; steering lock combined with ignition switch, starter and device to prevent accidental starter operation; lock on glove box.

"Hydraulic press-button system: Press-button hydraulic opening and closing of door windows; rear seat and center armrest fully adjustable hydraulically by pressing a button; front seats horizontally and vertically adjustable hydraulically by pressing a button; front backrest rake infinitely adjustable hydraulically down to horizontal position by pressing a button; hydraulic adjustment of shock-absorbers by lever.

"Heating and ventilating system: Front: heating and ventilating system with two heat-exchangers and blower; Rear: heating and ventilating system with one heat-exchanger and blower; fresh air system for front and rear; temperature selector with electronic control to compensate for effect of different driving speeds; defroster for side windows; defrosting for rear windows by electric heating elements embedded in the glass.

"Miscellaneous: Oddments tray between front seats; pockets on all four doors; parcel shelf in the front over transmission tunnel; parcel net on front seat backs; anti-dazzle rear view mirror; two exterior rear view mirrors adjustable from the inside; two padded sunvisors, with vanity mirror on passenger side; four handrails in the roof frame; grab-handles on all doors; four coat hangers in rear (two each side); armrests on all doors; independent centre armrest for each of the front seats; folding armrest in the rear; two adjustable headrests in the rear; ashtrays on all doors; automatic cigar lighter on all doors; safety steering wheel adjustable for rake; two foot rests in rear; curtains on rear window and rear side windows.

"Optional extras: Centre partition with hydraulically operated glass screen, bar, shelf for vanity box, and at right and left, folding tables with indirect lighting; steel sliding roof hydraulically operated by press-button."

Thomas returns and proceeds to show me how all these things work — and why: the engine with its twin alternators, the hydraulic system, the ventilated disc brakes with their doubled-up lines, the suspension — adjustable for both height and stiffness...

With all these overwhelming facts jammed into my head, I realize that the 600 is the ultimate expression of automotive perfection, the epitome of engineering virtuosity, workmanship, comfort and elegance. I also realize, with frustration, that no matter the words, no matter the pictures, my presentation will be inadequate — an entire book is needed to do the 600 justice!

But I am comforted by the thought that cars like the 540, the 300, the 600 — the likes of which we will never again see — are safe in the hands of men like Thomas Kreid, to whom the quest for perfection is not a mirage...

Of the 600 model, there were 2,677 units built. Of these, 428 were Pullmans. Of these, fifty-nine were Landaulets, and of these, seven were of the Presidential type — with the convertible top starting immediately behind the divider window, and otherwise equipped according to the special wishes of the customer. The example featured in these pictures belongs to Kenneth C. Smith of La Jolla, California. It was originally purchased by an Australian businessman. Other customers of Presidential Landaulets include Pope Paul, Queen Elizabeth, marshal Tito, and curiously, Chairman Mao. The price was in the eighty-thousand-dollar range — almost three times as much as a normally equipped Pullman.

280SE 3.5 CABRIOLET

The Man Who Preserves the Memories.

As a boy, Karl knew the river well. Every day he would watch the traffic on the Rhine: the long low-floating barges that came and went in a steady stream, the white yacht-like excursion ships, packed with tourists, and the small pleasure boats, sprinkled in-between like the beans in a boiling vegetable soup. Some were headed upstream toward Koblenz, working hard against the current, looking as if they were almost standing still. Others were headed downstream toward Cologne, floating swiftly, effortlessly.

Karl also knew the autobahn well. Every time he accompanied his father to Cologne or Bonn or Frankfurt he would watch the traffic: the long dark limousine-type cars that came roaring by in the fast lane, looking like express locomotives, their horns howling, and the low, smoothly shaped sports cars that appeared so suddenly in the rearview mirror, looking like small dots, and then, just as suddenly, had passed and were gone beyond the horizon, leaving only a memory to be stored away somewhere deep inside the brain.

Karl Keller was ten years old when the first Gullwings began to appear on German roads and highways. He was sixteen when Mercedes introduced the new beautiful 220SEb Coupes and Cabriolets. Three years later Karl had a car of his own, not yet a Mercedes, but an Opel — one time on the autobahn that year he drove the Opel as fast as it would go just for the pleasure of watching the exciting lines of a 300SL.

Also that year, 1964, Karl moved to America.

The 220SEb Coupes and Cabriolets were indeed new cars despite the fact that only a small "b" distinguished them from the earlier models. They were constructed according to the same principles as before,

but they now rested on a two-and-one-half-inch longer wheelbase and were also longer overall (eight inches), wider (about three inches), and lower (three inches).

When the 220SE Sedan was discontinued in 1959 the old Coupe and Cabriolet models were kept in production until the new ones were ready to take their places. But they were fitted with the updated engine, producing one hundred thirty-four horsepower. When the new Coupes and Cabriolets appeared in 1961, they were equipped with the same engine.

The new "b" model was fitted with disc brakes up front, which was an improvement over the earlier model and its drum brakes. Top speed was 107mph. Fourteen seconds were required to reach sixty.

If the 220SEb Coupes and Cabriolets were not entirely new under the skin, the skin itself was certainly brand new and very pleasing. It was a style that would last for a decade — another one of those Mercedes favorites that seem to vanish when they are at the height of their popularity. The trouble was that these cars were semi-handbuilt, particularly the Cabriolet with its padded top; nowadays, with automation and robot efficiency there does not seem to be room for the old-school craftsmen. Altogether nearly 36,000 units were built over the ten-year period.

The styling of the new model was a superb blend of traditional and modern lines. It had lost all the somewhat stodgy look of its predecessor, but was still just as elegant. The front end, especially when the less-cluttered, European-version headlights were fitted, was simple and slightly rounded. Without looking dated, it managed to carry on the traditional Mercedes theme — the classic radiator. The rear was also only slightly rounded with a smooth-ending fender line. The fins of the Sedan version were fortunately not incorporated into the styling of the new Coupe and Cabriolet. The front and rear ends harmonized extremely well. Two creases ran along the length of the body, tying the two ends together with long, sweeping lines. The interior, while lacking much of the wood of its predecessor, was still well enough appointed to be one of the most luxurious cars of its day, including cars that cost twice as much.

One thing the model always lacked was power! But something was done about that in 1963 when the 300SE came out with an enlarged engine, producing one hundred eighty horsepower. The 300SE had an air-suspension system and disc brakes all around. A chrome strip along the body side and around the wheel arches set that version apart from the regular model.

(continued on overleaf)

The 220SEb Coupe — as well as the subsequent 250 and 280 versions — were outstandingly beautiful automobiles. So classically timeless was the styling that it seemed just as appropriate at the time it was taken off the market in 1971, as it did when it was first shown a decade earlier. In 1969, with the introduction of the new 3.5 engine, a subtle styling change was made: The hood and grille were lowered three inches and the grille also widened four inches. Compare the two pictures, the 220 to the left, photographed in Baden-Baden, Germany, and the 3.5, above — subtle indeed! To the right, the comfortable reclining seats.

Some automobiles never become classics. Others have to wait a long time. The 1971 280SE 3.5 Cabriolet was an instant classic! The decade-old design already had the looks – mated with the new V-8, it also got the power and speed. Photographed on Chicago Tribune-founder Colonel Robert McCormick's estate in Wheaton, Illinois, this Survivor belongs to Karl Keller. He was assured by its first owner that the top had never been down. Keller always kept it that way – until it was lowered for the photographer. With 16,000 miles on the odometer, chassis number 111.027-12-001533, is certainly one of the most pristine examples to be found anywhere.

The injection system was improved in 1965 and a little more power was extracted. The model was built until the end of 1968.

When production of the 220SEb ended in 1965, the 250SE took over, now with a one hundred seventy horsepower engine. It was built until 1968 when the 280SE continued the theme. The engine was again more powerful, now one hundred eighty horsepower.

The final, and best, version came in 1969 when the all-new 3.5 vee-eight was dropped into the 280SE. Power was now up to two hundred thirty horsepower and top speed was 127mph. Zero to sixty took less than ten seconds. The hood was lowered to modernize the profile (made possible by the flatter engine). The radiator was also lowered (by about three inches) and widened (about four inches). Just then, 1971, when it was most desirable, production was halted — creating an instant classic!

Karl Keller went on to prove that America is indeed the land of opportunity. With the success of the company he started, came soon the resources necessary to realize a dream; he now has a garage full of Mercedes' best: Gullwings, Roadsters, a 600 and a pristine example of the 3.5 Cabriolet, which has only 16,000 original miles on the odometer and the top has never been down!

Pristine is the watchword! Karl is the sort of collector who insists on owning only the best — the perfect car of each model. He searches with extreme patience and miraculously seems to find that particular car nobody thought existed. When he has found the perfect example of the model he wants, he puts it away! He does not show his cars. He does not drive them — except for one, a 300SL Roadster he uses in his business when making sales calls on prospective customers.

When Karl puts his cars away, he puts them away — in an insulated garage that has a special system for keeping the temperature and the humidity at a constant level all year round. Inside the garage, all the cars have the proper covers, neatly stretched and spotless. There are also shields placed on the floor between the cars, behind each exhaust pipe, so that when he fires them up (on a regular basis), the car behind and its cover will not become stained. And to show how serious he is about not driving his cars, he built the garage without a driveway!

A childhood dream has come true for Karl Keller; owning the best of the best and keeping them that way forever!

(I forgot to ask him if he also collects Rhine river barges!)

The 280SE Cabriolet was certainly the last of the classic models from Mercedes-Benz. It was, to a large degree, handcrafted. And it had the kind of styling that expressed taste and affluence in an understated way. The photograph to the right, shows the basic Cabriolet body style in its 1962 300SE guise. Note the chrome strip that runs the length of the body side and the molding that follows the edge of the wheel arch. These are exterior clues to recognizing the top of the line of those early years. The flagship of the last of the line is recognized by the lower and wider grille, above, as well as what hides below the hood — the powerful 3.5, pictured to the left.

300SEL 6.3 SEDAN

The Six Point Three Illusion.

It was still raining when I came out from the Guggenheim Museum. I hesitated for a moment and then retreated to below the overhang. It looked like the shower was fizzling out, so I decided to stay where I was for a few minutes. The clouds of mist, whipped up by quickly passing buses and taxis, blurred my view of the naked-limbed dark-trunked trees in Central Park, rising on the other side of the street like a dead dripping jungle.

I rolled up the magazine I carried in my hand and stuck it safely inside my jacket. It was a special issue of *Road & Track*: the 1969 Road Test Annual. I had had a bite to eat in the museum coffee shop and afterward, since there had still been half an hour until my meeting with Peter Lewis, I had spent the rest of the time reading the magazine.

There were three road tests that interested me in particular. The first of those tests featured a car with a two-hundred-forty-cubic-inch vee-twelve producing four hundred horses. It covered zero to sixty in six point three seconds; zero to one hundred in fourteen point three. The top speed was one hundred sixty-three. The weight was well below three thousand pounds.

The car was a Lamborghini Miura.

The second test reported on a vee-eight with a three-hundred-twenty-seven-cubic-inch capacity producing three hundred fifty horses. It took seven point seven seconds to reach sixty; the zero-to-one-hundred time was not listed. The top speed was one hundred twenty-eight. Weight was about four hundred pounds more than the Miura.

(continued on overleaf)

The 300SEL 6.3 was first shown to a group of automotive journalists early in 1968. The photograph to the right, shows the fast sedan circling Germany's Hockenheim track during that press preview. To the left, the photographer has turned his camera to the instruments as the 6.3 nears top speed: 210 kmph. Note the speedometer needle! The hands on the wheel belong to none other than former team driver Karl Kling. Pictured above, are the proud parents, with their new child (from left to right): Uhlenhaut, responsible for engine and suspension; Scherenberg, in charge of overall development; Wilfert, responsible for styling.

Seemingly wanting to prove that, although they had chosen not to produce a true sports car any longer, the know-how was still there. Mercedes dropped the big 600-engine into a long sedan, creating the 300SEL 6.3 — a sedan so strong it could out-accelerate almost anything on the road. The 1971 Survivor shown here, chassis number 109.018-12-004623, belongs to Peter Lewis of Greenwich, Connecticut. It was photographed in front of an old granite garage on the family estate — a fitting backdrop for an elegant machine with subtle potency.

The car was a convertible Corvette.

The rain had stopped now. I left my refuge and started to walk down Fifth Avenue. Peter lived almost right across from The Metropolitan Museum of Art, further down on Fifth. It would take me awhile to cover the distance by foot but the air was cool and new-smelling and a brisk walk would do me good. Straight ahead I noticed that the turrets of the skyscrapers were hidden inside dark clouds.

There would soon be more rain.

The third car was also a vee-eight. The size was three hundred eighty-six cubic inches. It produced three hundred horses. Zero-to-sixty took six point nine seconds; about half a second slower than the Miura but almost one second faster than the Corvette. It weighed four thousand pounds; the heaviest of the three. Top speed was one hundred thirty-one; faster than the Corvette.

If the three of them had lined up for a quarter-mile drag contest there would have been very little separating them at the end of the race; the Miura would have covered the distance in fourteen point five seconds; the third car would have done it in fifteen point one seconds; the Corvette would have needed fifteen point six seconds.

The Miura had an extremely low body, sleek and posing very little air resistance. But it could seat only two people and it had very little room for luggage; about five cubic feet. The Corvette also had a low profile; it also held only two; its luggage space was less than seven cubic feet. The third car, on the other hand, could seat five people and there would still be lots of head and leg room, as well as about seventeen cubic feet of trunk space.

The third car was obviously not a sports car, even though the performance figures seemed to indicate so. It was in fact a sedan! The Mercedes-Benz 300SEL 6.3 Sedan! The best sedan in the world, according to *Road & Track!*

Now everything suddenly happened all at once; it started to rain again and I caught sight of Peter's metallic-gold 6.3 parked on the street in front of the canopy of the apartment building where he lives, and the doorman came out carrying my camera case that I had left with him earlier for safekeeping and behind him came Peter himself.

Peter Lewis is a super enthusiast. Super in the sense that his car interest covers a wider range than most. Super also in the sense that he owns more cars than most. Super, as well, in the sense that he is fortunate to be able to afford any car he desires.

Take Ferrari for instance. He has a Dino. And a 275

GTB/4. And a brand new black Boxer. Maybe also others. (Things could change between the writing of this story and the printing of the book!) Take another of his favorites, Mercedes-Benz. He has an old 300Sc Cabriolet that has been in the family since new. He has a 3.5 Cabriolet. He has an SLC. And, of course, he has the 6.3. (He has, in fact, had five of those). And take Aston Martin, yet another favorite. He has a Volante. And several others.

We enter the 6.3 as quickly as possible, trying to avoid getting wet. The doorman loads my camera case and Peter's briefcases in the trunk and we take off, heading north toward Greenwich, the water splashing around the tires, the rain drumming on the roof. Inside, the rich, dark brown leather seats smell like they should in a Mercedes; they also feel like they should — smooth from just the right amount of wear. The dash, walnut burl or South American Walnut — there are some dark swirls in it — shines rich and lustrous. We accelerate and decelerate, using the power of the engine and the power of the brakes to our advantage, darting in and out, occupying gaps in the traffic as they occur, avoiding both cars and potholes — there are too many of both in New York!

"Did you know this car will almost stay even with a Miura on the quarter-mile?" I ask Peter.

"I've never tried. But I believe you!" Peter says.

"It will beat a Corvette with a full second!"

"That I've tried!" Peter says with a wry smile. "They never seem to learn what those numerals on the rear deck lid stand for, do they?"

"What do you say is the reason for this incredible performance? Only the engine?" I ask Peter.

"The engine is it!" Peter answers. "They lifted it straight out of the big 600 and dropped it into the fifteen-hundred-pound-lighter 300. That engine was already a performer with the fuel injection and all. But in that lighter chassis... dynamite! I wish I could show you what this baby can do, but the roads are too wet! For instance... you cruise at twenty or thirty and suddenly stab the pedal... swish... the wheels spin... the tires smoke rubber! Maybe it won't rain in Greenwich so I can show you!"

"Let's hope it won't!" I say, now fully realizing the intriguing concept of the 6.3. "An illusion!" I add. "The car looks exactly like any other big Mercedes sedan, elegant and refined. But not showing, is a brute of an engine, so powerful it will beat most sports cars. And all that power is there for you to use as you choose. But only you know it. Marvelous!"

It did not rain in Greenwich...

The most powerful engine developed by Mercedes to date — for use in a production car — was the 6.3 unit, intended at first only for the magnificent 600 Limousine. The photograph above shows the unit in all its massive glory. When this engine was mated with the much lighter 300 Sedan, a most potent combination resulted — a combination that created the world's fastest production sedan. The photograph to the left, shows the engine compartment of the 300SEL, with the 6.3 unit fitted. To the right, a photograph of the instrument panel. Note the tachometer, small, but strategically located right in the center of the driver's field of view.

280SL ROADSTER

The Right Thing at the Right Time.

"Well, it was the last year of that body style," Andy says, giving me one of the reasons he added the 1971 280SL to his collection. "And it was also the last of the six-cylinder two-seaters," he says, pausing for a moment as if searching for words to express his feelings in a more profound way. "The 280SL was still built according to the old-time principles of excellence. You can see it in the choice of materials and in the way things were made and put together. I'm not saying that Mercedes isn't a great car today. But things are not the same now. The 280SL was the last of an era!"

Andy Cohn and I stand in front of the open doors of the ten-car garage he built a few years ago. Inside, in the back row, stand some thirties Fords. To the left sits a Ferrari Daytona Spyder, a Daytona Coupe and a Dino Spyder, all black — Andy likes dark cars. To the right stand other cars, all under cover — his company is the world's largest merchandiser of car covers. Straight ahead, just uncovered, its dark maroon surface sparkling from a recent polish, stands the 280SL.

Behind the garage the hill falls off steeply, straight down toward North Hollywood. On the other side, behind us, the hill slopes more gently, falling off gradually toward Beverly Hills.

Eight years ago, Andy, together with his partner Jim De Frank, decided on a joint venture; they bought an already well established auto parts store located on Robertson Boulevard in Beverly Hills, not far from Wilshire Boulevard.

Four years later they sold that business but kept the location and the building, opening Beverly Hills Motoring Accessories. As the name indicates, the company specializes in auto accessories, marketing them in all

(continued on overleaf)

The extremely unique photographs on these pages came from the camera of a certain Dr. Siefert, and were taken in the styling department at Mercedes-Benz. To the left, a one-to-ten-scale model in front of one of the first actual units to come off the assembly line. Note the vent on the model's side panel — similar to the one found on the 300SL! To the right, a comparison between the old 190SL and the new 230SL. Above, two one-to-ten-scale models beside a final full-scale model. Note the Mercedes-Benz script on the body side, behind the front wheel. The model closest to the camera, is the earliest, unpainted plaster version.

Replacement for the aging 190SL was the 230SL, arriving on the scene in 1963. It was an all-new design, with improved performance and with styling that matched its now firmly defined purpose of being a "sporty luxury automobile." In the subsequent 250SL and 280SL, engine capacity and performance grew further. This 1971 280SL, chassis number 113.044-12-022130, was photographed in front of the decorative French chateau facade of a private home in Los Angeles, California. Andy Cohn, co-founder of Beverly Hills Motoring Accessories, is the owner of this last-year-production Survivor – one o the best preserved examples you will ever find.

their various forms: everything from seats, covers, bras, wheels and exhaust systems to jewelry, watches, sun glasses and key fobs. The bulk of business comes from a nationwide mail order effort — most car enthusiasts are by now very familiar with their ads in *Road & Track.*

It turned out to be the right business at the right time. Interest in accessories soared during the past decade and the company has grown to become a leader in the field, thanks to high-quality products, personalized service and modern marketing techniques. The success of the company provides Andy with means to build a collection of his favorite cars.

"I searched a long time before I decided on this one," he says. "I wanted a last-year model. And I wanted a one-owner car, one with low mileage, and one that hadn't been repainted. I also wanted a dark color. This one has only thirty-three thousand miles on the odometer. It has never been parked in the sun, never been driven in the rain, and it has all the documents: original bill of sale, service records, manuals — everything — even the new-car sticker for the window. The car is just like it was when it left the showroom!

"I wouldn't have minded having one with the manual transmission," Andy continues. "But those cars are all run-down. The owners must drive them very hard! The five-speed is even more desirable. But you only find them in Europe. And all of them are rust-buckets!"

When the Mercedes development people began work on the car that would become the 230SL, they faced quite a challenge. It was clear from the outset that the 300SL could not, and was never meant to be, a big-volume seller. It was too much of a sports car. At its peak, in 1957, the 300SL Roadster was produced at an annual rate of five hundred units. For the rest of the run, annual production was about half that number. It was also clear that the 190SL was not all it should be. The main drawback was a lack of power. But the 190SL had proven one thing: the concept of a luxurious, rather than spartan and sporty looking, rather than sporty acting, two-seater was definately viable. At a seven-thousand-unit annual production rate, during its peak, the brother of the 300SL (or maybe more correctly, the sister), was a sales success.

So, the challenge facing the engineers and the stylists was that of creating a car that would occupy a position somewhere between the 190SL and the 300SL. But was it possible to please both the gentleman racer and the lady shopper? Was it possible to satisfy the need for superior handling at highway speed as well as for luxurious comfort at an urbane pace, for sparkling temperament as well as for dull flexibility?

When the 230SL arrived in 1963, it certainly seemed as if Uhlenhaut and his staff had hit the nail right on its head! The new car was indeed reminiscent of both its predecessors; it had the same wide, squat look and similar grille. But it was more elegant; finer, lighter looking. The unique element of the styling was the concave roof line of the hardtop. Like most styling innovations from Mercedes, this new look seems to have sprung from practical considerations: Structural strength was improved and larger windows and entrance openings were achieved. The interior was also more elegant than on its predecessors, imitating the style of the Sedans with their wide, comfortable seats.

Technically, the 230SL was no wonderchild. It was constructed according to the old proven ideas: unit frame and unit body. Although the improved swing axle was still used, the suspension had been carefully tuned to work with a new kind of tire, developed in cooperation with the manufacturers. The 230SL had drumbrakes in the back and discs up front; the 250SL got discs all around. The engine was the new six-cylinder unit, now slightly enlarged and producing one hundred fifty horsepower. Top speed was around 120mph. Zero to sixty took eleven seconds. The 280SL, which had an even more enlarged engine, producing one hundred seventy horsepower, made the zero-to-sixty run in just under ten seconds. All these performance figures were higher than those of the 190SL, but lower than those of the 300SL — right on target!

During the eight years of production 26,000 units of the 190SL were built. Of the 230SL, 250SL, 280SL, twice as many were made, also during an eight-year period — another bull's-eye for Mercedes!

But a curious thing happened over the years. When the 230SL was first introduced, its sporty character was emphasized. It was even winning tough rallys — a well publicized fact. And indeed, in the beginning the 230SL was driven by a more sporty clientéle. But then came women's liberation — and the car that helped that movement along was the little roadster from Mercedes! How could the Mercedes officials have been so far-sighted? (Just in case someone thinks I'm serious: I'm not!)

"I wouldn't go as far as to say that the 280SL is a feminine car!" says Andy. "All you have to do is to drive it closer to the limit than most drivers do and you will discover the tremendous response of the engine and the superior grip on the road. I would say that the 280SL is a car for the sophisticated man as well as for the liberated woman!" adds Andy with a wink.

The right car for the right time!

The photographs on these pages, also from the camera of Dr. Seifert, show the interior styling of one of the pre-production models on display in the styling department at Mercedes-Benz. To the left, a suggestion for a third, transversally located, passenger seat. This picture also shows a different design of the backs of the normal seats. To the right, two suggestions for design of the door panel with its map pocket. Above, the instrument panel. Note that, at this stage, there were still areas of variation from the final product: the shape of the fresh-air outlet, the location of the clock, the design of the heating and ventilation controls, etc.

450SL ROADSTER

Of New and Old, of Good and Bad.

The orange trees stand ripe with fruit. It is the richest harvest in years and the branches bear it out, hanging heavy and full. The oranges look like bright stars sprinkled across a lush, green heaven. The groves extend from the road, spreading their endless abundance on both sides of it, and, looking at them from the car, the nearest rows of trees appear blurred because of the speed. It all feels very pleasant and rich and blessed, and I press down hard on the gas pedal causing the front to raise, the speed to surge, the car to accelerate briskly along the straightaway leading out of Fillmore and up into the mountains.

I am driving Bob Scudder's light-green 450SL. Bob sits beside me in the passenger seat. We had taken off the hardtop before starting out this morning, leaving it hanging from the rafters in Bob's garage. The soft top was off too, neatly stowed away underneath its lid, behind us. The crisp spring air, laced with the intoxicating fragrance of the citrus flowers, comes rushing past us in the open cockpit. The day's shooting is over and I can relax now, letting my senses settle down to enjoy the feel of the car on the road.

"First time I've driven a 450SL!" I say as I prepare for an approaching turn, a left-hander, the first of many turns, the road beginning to climb the mountainside now, winding in and out of steep-walled ravines, looking like the long body of a snake. "I'm really impressed!" I add, turning my head just enough to register Bob's contented smile.

The Mercedes sweeps around the corner in a smooth, stable, predictable manner. Moving out of the curve, I press the gas pedal again, feeling the tires dig into the road surface.

"I'm also surprised!" I say. "I thought it would feel more like the 280SL!"

(continued on overleaf)

The 450SL had an all-new interior; only the classic star in the center of the steering wheel revealed that the car was a Mercedes. There was nothing else left of the style that had characterized the cars from the world's oldest car maker for so many years: the wooden dash, the leather and wood combination, or the leather and steel. That is not to say that all was lost; the new interior was an excellent design, from a viewpoint of styling as well as ergometrics. Above, the 450SL from its best angle, and to top it off, the simple, good-looking European-style headlight covers. To the right, a comparison between new and old — the blood line is evident!

By 1971, the time had come to replace the 280SL – the 450SL was the machine to do it! It still carried forward the theme of "sporty luxury automobile," but it now looked even sportier thanks to the steeply raked windshield and the sleeker overall lines. Bob Scudder of Camarillo, California owns this well-preserved 1973 450SL, chassis number 107.044-12-011142, photogaphed in front of the church built by the Camarillo brothers in the early part of the century. One of the most desirable years to a California collector is 1973 – last year for the small bumpers.

"No! The 450SL is really quite different!" Bob says emphatically. "It's a new car all the way. Styling too. Obviously!"

"I like the feeling behind the wheel!" I say. "The driving position is excellent. Feels more sporty than the 280SL. I'm not talking about driving characteristics now. I'm talking about environment. It's the raked windshield that does it. And the big console between us here. It feels like I'm sitting deeper. More encapsulated. I like that! Yes, the 450SL is definately more sporty than the 280SL. But not as elegant!"

"I agree!" says Bob. "That is true for the overall styling, too. Sportier. But not as elegant."

"They carried that pagoda-like roof line over to the new hardtop, though," I say, letting the steering wheel slide back through my hands after a sharp right-hander. "But it doesn't seem as tall as on the 280SL. I always thought that roof was too tall! The entire car looks rounder and heavier. Especially the body sides and the hood. The rear deck lid, on the other hand, is slightly concave, repeating the roof line. The fact that the rear wheel arch is cut so low makes the car appear even heavier. Another thing, quite nice I think, is the ribbing below the doors. It's not there for looks. Is that right?"

"Yes, that's right!" Bob says. "Like everything else Mercedes does, it has a function. It's supposed to affect the airflow so that the side windows are kept clean from dirt and water when it rains. Same thing with the ribbing on the rear lights, I understand!"

"Overall, I think it's a very good looking car!" I say. "A classy looking car!" I add. "But not a *great* looking car! A matter of taste, of course!"

"Yes, those things are sometimes hard to discuss. One thing though, it does look like a Mercedes. The traditional relationship is there!"

"Yes, the Mercedes stylists are good at that. Always have been!" I say. "But the interior is quite a departure from old. No wood on the dash anymore. And no leather. It's plastic now. I feel bad about that. Not genuine. Look at this!" I point at the door panel "Fake stitches! But at least all the pieces fit well together. The workmanship is still tops. And the instrumentation is great. I like the way the upper half of the steering wheel is empty, leaving an unobstructed view of the gauges, and the way the instrument pod is styled, repeating the shape of the opening in the steering wheel. That's very good!"

I am moving in and out of the curves now, the road rising steadily. I am not driving hard, not pushing it, just letting the car flow with the road — the 450SL performs superbly. The ride is smooth and even. The steering is

The 450SLC — the four-seater coupe version of the 450SL — was introduced at the same time and in the same place as its shorter brother — the 1971 Geneva show. It rested on a fourteen-inches-longer wheelbase, and was also longer overall with the same measurement — evidence that a section had simply been added behind the seats of the 450SL. The louvres mounted inside the rear quarter windows set the SLC apart from the SL, at the same time as it gave the SLC a more elegant appearance. Under the hood, pictured to the right, they were both the same.

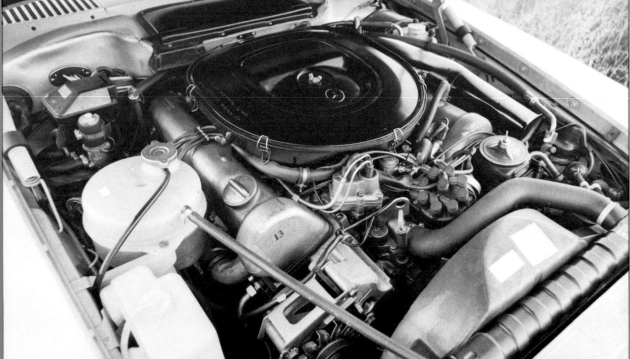

practically neutral. The resistance in the wheel feels absolutely perfect.

"The handling must be the greatest improvement over the 280SL," I say. "It's fabulous!"

"Yes, they finally got rid of that swing axle!" Bob says. "They have semi-trailing arms now."

"What about the transmission?"

"New too. It's a three-speed automatic with torque converter. Very smooth. They were never imported with manual transmission."

"And the engine?" I ask. "I know it's a vee-eight. But what about performance?"

"The engine was new too. In Europe, they brought it out as a 3.5. But for America, with those emission laws and all, the engine was fitted with a taller block so that the stroke could be longer. But still, power was about the same in both cases. About two hundred horses. Acceleration was down a little compared to the 280SL."

"Too bad it had to be that way."

Bob Scudder grew up in Washington, Indiana. He can trace his interest in cars back to the time when his father took him to see the factory in Evansville, where they assembled the Plymouth Fury. Later, when that time came, he decided to study mechanical engineering.

The 450SL was Bob's first Mercedes. He looked at seventeen of them before he decided on this one. A real-estate saleswoman in Lancaster had owned it before. She had only driven it nineteen thousand miles. Bob specifically wanted a '73 model — because of the small bumpers.

Mercedes ownership soon turned into more than a passing interest; Bob became a co-founder of the Channel Islands Section of the Mercedes-Benz Club of America, its first vice president and its second president. Luckily, Bob's wife, Charlene, shares her husband's interest.

During their years as 450SL owners, other Mercedes cars have come and gone; a 190SL, a 280SE, a 250SE Coupe, a 300SEL 6.3 . . . They have now purchased a beautifully restored 220SEb Coupe. It is going to be their show car. The 450SL will remain their roadcar.

We reach the summit now and begin to roll down the other side of the mountain, the road still undulating, the view now displaying another green paradise of orange groves, and, in the distance, the soft outline of Anacapa Island, its blue-gray contour floating heavy on the fuzzy horizon of the Pacific. We both sit quietly, enjoying the downhill rush, the slow gyration, the flowing wind . . .

"I can understand why you want to keep this one for your road car!" I say. "Few cars I have driven would have felt so good going down this hill!"

"Mercedes for the Road," eighth in The Survivor Series, was photographed, written and designed by Henry Rasmussen. The technical specifications, the brief history and the notes on collectability were compiled by Gene Babow. All black and white photographs, unless otherwise indicated, were obtained from **Road & Track**, mainly from their Studio Wörner Collection. Librarian Otis Meyer provided valuable help in locating the material. Assistant designer was Walt Woesner. Copy editor was Barbara Harold. Typesetting was supplied by Tintype Graphic Arts of San Luis Obispo, California. The color separations were produced by South China Printing Company of Hong Kong, which was responsible for printing and binding as well. Liaison man with the printer was Peter Lawrence of New York City.

Special acknowledgements go to Jose Harth and his family of Caracas, Venezuela, for making the author's stay there an unforgettable experience; to Bill Kosfeld of Motorbooks International for his pleasant handling of day-to-day contacts connected with publishing. The author is also indebted to Tom Warth of Motorbooks International, whose continued support made yet another title in this series possible.

The author finally wishes to thank the following contributors: Frank Barrett, editor and publisher of **The Star** magazine, Charles Brahms, Paul Dexler, Bob Esbensen, Jobst Heemeyer, John Harrington, Bruce Meyer, Ena Rasmussen, Robert Reinfried, Shirley Rusch, Paul Russell of the Gullwing Service Company, Topsfield, Massachusetts, John Sheetz, Frank Skinner and Kenneth Smith.